OTHER BOOKS BY ROBERT T. FRANCOEUR

The World of Teilhard de Chardin, 1961

Perspectives in Evolution, 1965

Evolving World, Converging Man, 1970

Utopian Motherhood:
    New Trends in Human Reproduction, 1970

Eve's New Rib:
    Twenty Faces of Sex, Marriage, and Family, 1972

Edited by Robert T. and Anna K. Francoeur
The Future of Sexual Relations, 1974

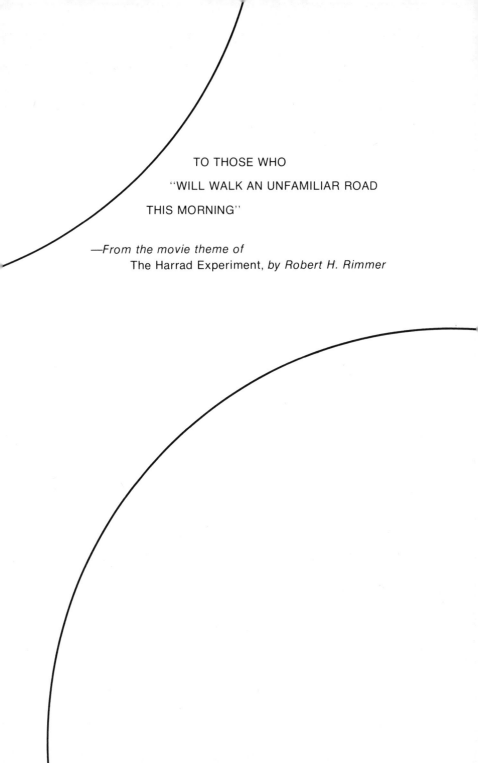

TO THOSE WHO

"WILL WALK AN UNFAMILIAR ROAD

THIS MORNING"

—*From the movie theme of*
   The Harrad Experiment, *by Robert H. Rimmer*

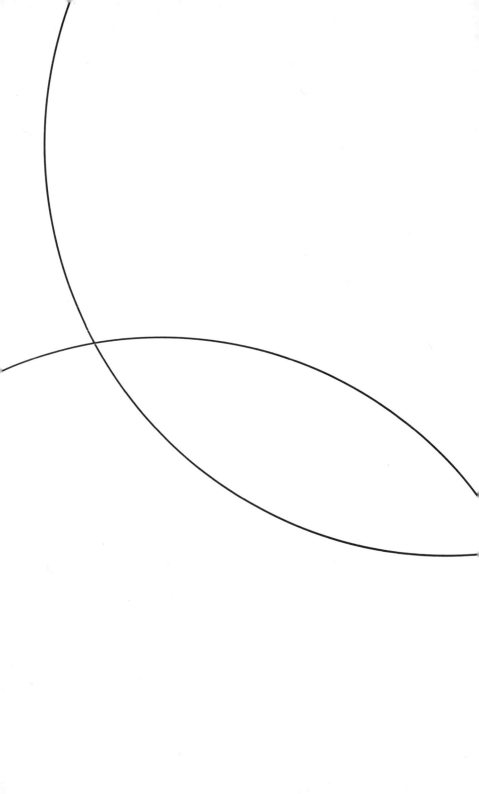

HOT & COOL SEX
Cultures in Conflict

By Anna K. and Robert T. Francoeur

Introduction by Robert H. Rimmer

HARCOURT BRACE JOVANOVICH

NEW YORK · LONDON

Printed in the United States of America

Library of Congress Cataloging in Publication Data
Francoeur, Anna K
    Hot and cool sex.

    Bibliography: p.
    1. Sex.   2. Marriage.   3. Interpersonal relations.
4. Family.   I. Francoeur, Robert T., joint author.
II. Title.   [DNLM: 1. Sex.   2. Sex behavior.   HQ21
F825h]
HQ12.F7   301.41   74-10984
ISBN 0-15-142173-0

First edition

B C D E

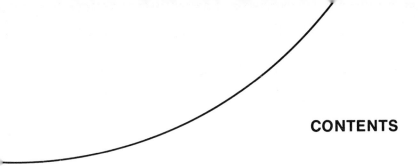

CONTENTS

PART THREE: TRANSITIONS

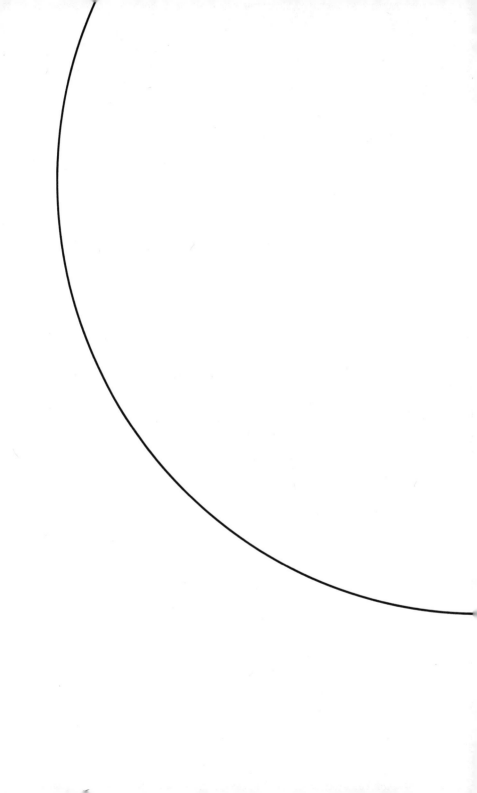

INTRODUCTION
By Robert H. Rimmer

I don't know whether it happens to many novelists, but occasionally I discover real-life people who both visually and in their approaches to life are doubles for fictional characters I have written about. This fascinates me because more often than not I do not write with a particular person in mind, but tend to project into some characters the kind of person I would enjoy knowing, if he or she existed.

In my novel *Proposition 31,* one of the two couples who eventually merge their families is Horace and Tanya Shea. Horace is a professor at the California Institute of Sociology (fictitious), and his wife, Tanya, is an advertising artist with her entire training in the commercial world. They have two boys, Mitch and Sam. Tanya's background is Scandinavian. Like Anna Francoeur, she is direct, pragmatic, with a no-nonsense point of view on the realities of survival in a capitalistic society. Horace, like Bob Francoeur, is the dreamer, the utopianist, the cross-culturist, the man who can bridge knowledge in different disciplines and reveal striking parallels. Seemingly opposite, Tanya and Horace reinforce each other.

Being pretty certain that the photographs of Anna and Bob Francoeur, and the publisher's descriptions that will grace this book, will not give the full "flavor" of the Francoeurs, I want to tell you a little bit more about Anna and Bob. Although I didn't meet them until several years after *Proposition 31* was published, for me they were Horace and Tanya come to life—curious, captivatingly enthusiastic, wondrous, and filled with a belief "that man will prevail."

Instead of two boys, Anna and Bob have Danielle and Nicole, two young daughters, who, like their father and mother, seem to be opposite sides of the same coin. As I gradually became acquainted with Anna and Bob, I kept thinking they would be wonderful candidates for a group marriage, especially Anna, who has a cool, capable Middle European peasant style that was unfortunately lost by millions of women in the powder-and-lace urban environment of the eighteenth and nineteenth centuries. Long before the advent of the Hot Sex era, Anna—I believe in reincarnation—would have plowed the fields with her man, gotten pregnant by him before she married him, and gone to bed with him in a calm, joyful, egalitarian sexual relationship. Keep in mind, as Anna and Bob point out in this book, that many of the Hot Sex attitudes of the cities and even of religion only partially penetrated the lower-income class of society, which included the tillers of the soil.

Which is to say that Anna past, and Anna present, is a liberated woman, and this kind of female requires a whole new learning experience for the male. How this evolved between Anna and Bob, and their marriage itself, is a fascinating story I hope they will tell someday. But, for the reader of this book, I think it is important to know that it is an ongoing search for values and questioning of "reality" that you would experience with the Francoeurs if you could know them personally. As you read, think of the experience as a rambling walk through the history of man's interpersonal and sexual relationships, with Anna and Bob, your guides, sometimes agreeing with each other and sometimes disagreeing, and then, at points where you may think they have gone too far, calmly stopping short and asking: "What would you do? What would your solution be?" Abraham Maslow wrote this way, and the style has a kind of insidious intrigue, because you slowly realize, as you are being led along, that you aren't being proselytized, but, rather, presented with a landslide of observations on the human scene. If you disagree with their conclusions, that's all right. The important thing is that *you* are involved in the creative thinking process and in an interaction between reader and author that, in the case of this book, at least, disproves McLuhan's thesis and offers you the printed word as a cool, involving medium.

One of the important things this kind of book does for me—and I'm sure that hundreds of thousands of readers will discover the same kind of dialogue with Anna and Bob—is that over and over again it catalyzes my thinking. For example, a few years ago I first came across the concept of "knowing" another human being explained in its Biblical sense by Bob in his book *Utopian Motherhood.* This is now covered in much more detail, in its Cool Sex sense—"knowing" as a completely communicated relationship that includes the act of sexual intercourse in its gestalt.

Back in 1935, when I was in college, I not only took courses in Greek, hoping ultimately, for no particular reason except the joy of it, to be able to read the New Testament in its primary language, but I also took a course in the Old Testament given by a then nationally famous Biblical scholar and practicing minister. I have no recollection that "knowing" another human being in the Hebraic, *yahdah* meaning of the word was ever mentioned in that course—in fact, I'm sure it wasn't. For the most part, even the bubbling sexuality of the Old Testament, already much subdued in the King James translation, was ignored by this upright teacher in favor of the historical authenticity of the various documents.

Now, that was really sad. Because in those days I and many of my peers were in love in a Hot Sex kind of way that wasn't really reflecting our innate idealism and our feeling that a particular friend of the other sex was much more a snuggly human being than a sex object. And, of course, some of us in those days had "gone steady" long enough to have inveigled the girl, if not into bed (it wasn't easy to find a private one in those days), at least into the back seat of an automobile, where we valiantly tried to merge our genitals. And when it was over, I'm sure in my own case, at least, if the girl and I had been able to express the imagery of knowing, we would have been aware that the postcoitum *tristesse,* and the inadequacy of my ejaculation and her orgasm (if she achieved it at all), could have been summed up in our failure to know one another. But, of course, if that Biblical professor had realized that education in religion and education in good interpersonal and sexual relationships are not incompatible, but actually closely related subjects, the 1930's would have been an entirely different kind of premarital world.

Thus, long after I had written *The Harrad Experiment,* I discovered in Bob's book an important collective verb that in many ways sums up the kind of interpersonal, being-naked-with-you style of life that my characters and I, personally, delight in. In this book I have made many similar discoveries: "knowing" in this Biblical sense exemplifies Cool Sex; and *maithuna,* extended sexual intercourse, which I have extolled as a form of communication in practically every novel I have written, likewise appears here under the Cool Sex umbrella. And, of course, this entire extended development of McLuhan and Leonard's Hot and Cool Sex concepts incorporates and expands, as Anna and Bob show, the O'Neills' Closed and Open Marriages, and Taylor's Matrist and Patrist societies, thus providing an illuminating framework in which we can evaluate the sexual history of man. With very little stretching of the imagination, the Cool Sex approaches to living described and elaborated by the Francoeurs in this book could become a manifesto for what remains of the New Left, giving the activists of the late 1960's (and those of us who still believe in the greening of America and that some form of Consciousness III is still very much alive) a political approach that is closely related to the life styles of what will inevitably include a majority of Americans. Let the politicians take heed. Cool Sex in the microcosm will shake the foundations of politics in the macrocosm.

Lest you think that I am, unqualifiedly, agreeing with all of Anna's and Bob's views in this book, let me assure you that for me (and I hope for you) the learning process, in any good book, emerges both as you agree and as you argue with the author. For example, in the chapter "Fidelity Today," Anna and Bob contend that "the prolonged adolescence of American youth, with its extended courtship and dating pattern, provides a world in which they can gradually explore and develop competence and skill in physical communication," and they continue: "With a diffused degenitalized sexuality, today's youth are free to explore at their own pace the intimacies of holding hands and fond glances, petting and fondling, and the more committed modes of genital communication."

Being somewhat Skinnerian, I have come to the conclusion that Cool Sex must, and can, be taught. If the Harrad idea ever prevails, then, of course, the prolonged adolescence would stop at seventeen, and youngsters would live together in close intimacy and make love together, unmarried, in a socially open learning milieu where they experience, as part of their premarital environment, more than one member of the other sex. My theory is that mutual or lonely masturbation is not so cool or so sound a part of the education process as having sexual intercourse with a friend of the other sex, or simultaneously having teachers who are friends to lean upon. Also, I might not fully agree with Anna's and Bob's conclusions on Sandstone, but I am fascinated by them, as you will be.

I could write more about the chemistry of this book on my mind and yours, but you shouldn't delay. Something nice is about to happen to you. You are about to make two new friends. Begin now, preferably with a pen in hand, so you can scribble in the margins and have a cool, interacting dialogue with Anna and Bob—or, if you get charged up enough, then write to them. I'm sure they'll answer you!

PART ONE
IMAGES AND MODELS

1. SEX AND COMMUNICATIONS: UTILITY VS. AESTHETICS

Now Adam knew *his wife, and she conceived.*
—Genesis 4:1

We do not yet know *what it means to be male or female in this brave new world.*
—ROBERT T. FRANCOEUR, *Eve's New Rib*

Four and a half million Americans get married each year. Roughly 150 million Americans are married today.

On the other hand, 660,000 divorces were granted to Americans in 1969. In 1971, the number was 768,000. With "no-fault" divorce laws becoming effective in some states, over 851,000 divorces were granted between February 1972 and February 1973. By early 1973 the divorce rate in some western states was over 70 per cent of the marriage rate. More than 12 per cent of all American men and 14 per cent of all American women have been married twice.

One hardly needs these statistics to confirm one's own awareness that the traditional marriage and family are facing serious problems. Nor is there much hope in the analyses of countless sociologists, psychologists, and other experts who have concentrated on some fairly obvious external social factors, such as economic shifts, effective contraceptives, women's liberation, increased social mobility, affluence, and leisure. Undoubtedly these social factors have been a major influence in forcing changes in marriage patterns. Technology has always created its own social structures and cultural patterns. We cannot underrate the external social factors, but we do not want to stop there. The prime effect of these outside social forces rests in the shadows of our consciousness. The basic issue, we are convinced, is a radical shift in our personal understanding and appreciation of ourselves and others as sexual persons.

External factors have produced a tense, still-unresolved revolution in our consciousness, a basic evolution in our sexual imagery. Along with our changing understanding of what it means to be male and female, there is a revolution in the traditional appreciation of intimacy, responsibility, and fidelity in human relations. The eye of the storm is a new way in which men and women relate to one another as sexual persons. New attitudes, values, and expectations are evolving.

The difficulty we have in pinning down this shift in consciousness does not reduce its reality. Every single person and every married couple in this country feel the tensions created by the new sexual images. Naturally, each of us experiences this tension in his own way, some intensely, some vaguely. But in each case the nucleus of the revolution is the same.

Many analysts have offered interpretations of the radical alteration in our understanding of ourselves as sexual persons by focusing on the changing uses of sexual relations. Sex, in the words of British biologist Alex Comfort, is now "elaborated into a key force in shaping the development of human personality and behavior." Bed is the best place to play all the games one ever wanted to play, according to Hugh Hefner. Sex is for fun, for one's pleasure, for giving pleasure, for supporting one's ego, for asserting one's masculinity or affirming one's femininity. Always sex for something, which leaves us with the image of human sexuality as a tool. This pragmatic, utilitarian approach is quite different from the aesthetic, contemplative image of human sexuality expressed simply in the Biblical phrase "Now Adam knew his wife."

Sex is not for communications. It is communication. It is not a way of relating. It is relating. If we use sex as a means to an end, it is cut off from the real essence of our lives. It becomes something out there, for procreation, an ascetic key to heaven, for pleasure. When sex is integrated into the personality, the spotlight formerly on the genital tool diffuses over the whole human person. Human sexuality becomes communicative, contemplative, polymorphic and aesthetic.

Some commentators have touched on this shift in sexual consciousness, but without exploring in depth the changing attitudes, values, and expectations that necessarily accompany such a metamorphosis from utilitarian to aesthetic sex. The most helpful insights have come from two visionary analysts of communications, George B. Leonard and Marshall McLuhan. Leonard, a former senior editor of *Look* magazine, provokes his readers to new insights by bringing together in unusual combinations fascinating but little-known facts from the history of human sexual attitudes. His books include *Education and Ecstasy, The Transformation,* and *The Man and Woman Thing and Other Provocations.* McLuhan, of course, is known for testing traditional images by twisting our comfortable, clearly defined words into new shapes and meanings. In 1967 the two joined forces briefly in an article, "The Future of Sex," for *Look* magazine. In this perceptive analysis of our evolving sexual attitudes, they created the social myth of "Hot and Cool Sex." In terms of understanding where we have been and where we might be heading, "Hot and Cool Sex" provides a fascinating and rich perspective. In our book we will try to develop and extend this seminal model.

As a backdrop for our exploration of Hot and Cool Sex, we need to review some of the basic themes in McLuhan's over-all analysis of communications. One is that modes of communication have become more important than their content. This major revolution in communications media, this shift from printed words to electronic signals, triggers an even more radical revolution in our culture. Technologies create unique brands of cultures. Television, McLuhan argues, is wooing us away from our thousand-year-old love affair with the dogmatic printed word and the linear book. He sets in opposition the civilized detachment of the literate man and the total involvement of the nonliterate person who relies on instantaneous oral communications. The whole human race, in McLuhan's vision, is being "retribalized," consolidated into a tribal culture on a global scale, by the instantaneous omnipresent eye of the television camera and screen. This now common mode of communications creates a structural revolution in society, as well as a revolution in values.

In *Understanding Media: The Extensions of Man,* McLuhan explains his distinction between hot and cool media. "A hot medium is one that extends one single sense in 'high definition.' High definition is the state of being well filled with data. A photograph is, visually, 'high definition.' A cartoon is 'low definition,' simply because very little visual information is provided." The photograph, in a way, excludes the viewer. Its clear detail rules out participation. What can one possibly add to its already complete image? The cartoon, on the other hand, invites participation with its rough incomplete outlines. Printed books and lectures are hot communications media because they do not invite participation. A seminar discussion, on the other hand, is a cool medium because it requires involvement.

Many critics have bristled at McLuhan's use of "hot" and "cool." Admittedly, his use of these adjectives is novel and confusing, especially to people who love the clarity of the printed word. But his heterodox use of words can be provokingly helpful when one is dealing with concepts that do not fit traditional patterns.

When McLuhan speaks of hot and cool communications he is concerned with the media more than with the content. "The medium is the message." But when he joins with Leonard to speak of hot and cool sexual consciousness, most of the emphasis is on content. As modes of communicating different sexual attitudes and values (content), one can contrast the well-defined Hot Sex images, or media, of Raquel Welch, Ursula Andress, or the *Penthouse* and *Playboy* centerfolds with the low definition of today's unisex clothes and hair styles, which often render male and female indistinguishable. However, when one moves beyond these visual media, it becomes awkward to suggest that motels, the back seats of cars, affairs, and mistresses are Hot Sex media, while water beds, multimedia light shows, Woodstock–

Watkins Glen festivals, and group marriages are Cool Sex media.

The adjective *hot* invariably carries with it overtones of something vital, stimulating, filled with life, while the word *cool* leaves us with the image of something passionless, uninspiring, dull, and lifeless. Carried over into the area of human sexual relations, these traditional connotations are uncomfortable because they distort the McLuhan-Leonard models of Hot and Cool Sex.

Applied to our changing awareness of human sexuality and the "retribalization" of sexual mores, Hot and Cool Sex are untried and undefined concepts. In their 1967 *Look* article McLuhan and Leonard barely sketched the broad outlines. McLuhan has not, to our knowledge, returned to the subject, and Leonard only briefly, in his book *The Transformation.* Our own interest in developing the promises of the Hot and Cool Sex models has grown over the past six years. At first we were very cautious because of our skepticism about oversimplified models. But the enthusiastic agreement our tentative discussions of Hot and Cool Sex stirred encouraged us to work out the distinction in fuller detail. What we offer here is the result of our efforts: a portrait of Hot and Cool Sex attitudes, with a study of their expression in two common forms of marriage—closed and open—where the meanings of intimacy and jealousy, commitment and fidelity are set in sharp contrast. Finally, we hope to offer some useful guidelines for coping with the tensions and conflicts involved in the transformation in sexual attitudes.

Before we move into these areas, we would like to say a few words about the mythic reality of both Hot and Cool Sex. We say "mythic reality" on purpose. Hot and Cool Sex really exist, but they also do not exist. The traditional Hot Sex romantic marriage has been an ideal, a social myth that has guided several generations of Americans. Yet few people could put into words the attitudes, values, and expectations of this social model. The Cool Sex consciousness is also as unreal as it is real. Because of its cartoonlike low definition, we have been forced to create a composite portrait, drawing on certain real elements anthropologists have noted in various tribal cultures past and present.

In one sense, our image of Cool Sex may sound like a romanticized nostalgia for a lost Eden. Just as modern technology and Western civilization are turning our last so-called primitive cultures into fossils, modern man seems compelled to romanticize his sexual attitudes and consciousness, weaving them into a new mythic pattern. The result is a real-unreal synthesis of attitudes and images distilled from the real past but including some visionary personal projections. Cool Sex, as we have developed it here, is not a nostalgia for some lost Eden, but, rather, a mythic symbol of a new image of human sexuality, rooted in the past and flowering in the future.

The shift from hot to cool communications media creates a revolution in our social structures, images, and values. A similar revolution is in progress as we shift from Hot Sex to Cool Sex images and values. Aesthetics is replacing utility, at first subconsciously, but then, it is to be hoped, with a fuller awareness of where we are headed in human relations.

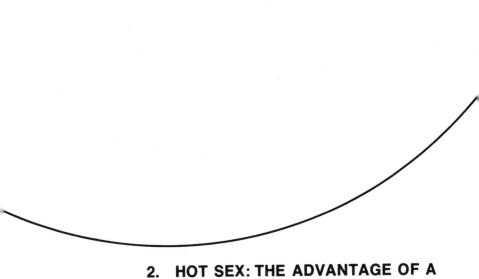

2. HOT SEX: THE ADVANTAGE OF A FORMIDABLE WEAPON

Those who are hit hardest by change are those who imagine that it has never happened before.
—ELIZABETH JANEWAY, *Man's World, Woman's Place*

"She stared at it in wonder. *'C'est formidable. Un vrai canon.'* "

This exquisite Hot Sex compliment was uttered by Loren Hardeman's French playmate in Harold Robbins' Hot Sex novel, *The Betsy.* Loren Hardeman I, industrial magnate, is aggressive, brutal, competitive—a tyrannic patriarch whose very surname bears witness to his Hot Sex lineage and values.

The essence of our Hot Sex culture is sex, meaning genital interlocking and nothing else. Hot Sex is isolated from everyday life, confined to the groins. Hardeman's French maid judged him as a male by the impressive size of his penis. And he judged her as a female by her anatomical endowments: bursting bust, buttocks, and genitals on display.

The concept of Hot Sex, in keeping with its McLuhan-Leonard communications-model analogy, has high definition. Its values, expectations, concerns are easily defined because the Hot Sex mentality chooses to simplify things by reducing the mysteries of human sexuality to disembodied genitals. A Hot Sex society, in Irving Buchen's sardonic view, "treats a man or a woman solely as a series of anal, oral and genital orifices to be filled, exhausted, emptied or violated."

Human sexuality is segmented from life because we fear it. Unable to accept it as an integrated part of our lives, we schedule, arrange, and plan it, in both time and place: the comfortable secrecy of the dark night, the privacy of the bedroom, the plotted affair with its games and role playing. A Hot Sex mentality simplifies the varied emotions and sense feelings in the man-woman relationship by leaving them off-stage. This genital upstaging is so common in our culture that we assume automatically that a man and a woman cannot be close and intimate without ending up in bed.

In a Hot Sex culture, it is easy to define a man or woman. The eternal, unchanging stereotypes surround us with monotonous casts: the faceless he-man, superstud, athlete, breadwinner, and head of the household, aggressive, competitive, and protective of the equally faceless aproned housewife, the diaper-radiant mother, sentimental, romantic, submissive, and needing protection. In everyday life, the roles are often far more real than the individuals impersonating them.

Women have no identity. They exist as relative creatures whose functions and behavior are defined in terms of man's needs and wants. Hot Sex values relate men to women in much the same way philosophers have pictured the relationship of soul and body, the active element, male, or soul, giving life and form to the passive object, woman, or body. In this framework woman is an object to be abused for man's carnal pleasure or used as an instrument for procreation. In the quick phrase of Howard theologian Rosemary Ruether, Hot Sex is "the Puritan-Prurient Syndrome of the coldly instrumental or the dirty." In a patriarchal system the male must be the active partner, dominating by brute strength and rational logic the female, whose virtues are those of passivity, obedience, dependence.

Woman's position as an object puts her in the unique situation of a possession, property. In marriage a man acquires a housekeeper, a nursemaid for himself and his progeny, and a plaything. The bride is "given away" by the father. No groom, however immature, has ever been given away. In marriage the wife trades her surname for her husband's family name. She becomes "Mrs. George Smith."

A nationally known television personality expressed this property relationship succinctly when he interrupted Bob's attempt to contrast Open Marriage, including our concept of satellite relations, with the traditional marriage. With deep emotion, he cried, "I'll strangle the bastard who puts his paws on my property!" Despite all protests to the contrary, women today are still restricted in what they can do on their own authority. The property relationship may be waning, but it is far from gone. In practice our society still finds it more comfortable to follow the advice of the Epistles of Paul, in which women are seen as irrational, unpredictable, and sensual creatures who should gratefully accept male guidance.

By and large the property status of women benefits men. In work and recreation, society allows women considerable independence and self-determination. But in other areas, especially social, they are limited. Our Hot Sex culture assumes that married couples exist as asexual packaged units. We find it difficult to cope socially with a wife attending a public function without her husband. And we find it a tense situation when a wife unexpectedly arrives at a dinner party accompanied by a male other than her husband.

In this same property framework, virginity, adultery, and fornication represent moral values designed primarily for the female. In earlier times the father's concern about his daughter's virginity was tied in with the economic factor: bride prices depended on the quality of goods. The new husband had to be sure no other male had tampered with the incubator in which he intended to sow his seed. After marriage the husband was concerned about the legitimacy of his heir and sufficient progeny to help with the field work and comfort his old age. The legal status of women as property and the economics of virginity were neatly stated in an early-seventh-century Kentish law: "If a man forcibly carries off a maiden, he shall pay fifty shillings to her owner and afterwards buy from the owner his consent."

Hot Sex cultures are curiously haunted by the virginity complex, probably as a result of an attraction-repulsion conflict. Attraction and fear collide in the male's desire to be the first to deflower a maiden and his dread that some other male may have deflowered his new property. Not unexpectedly, this property status does not apply to the autonomous male. In fact, male virginity is frowned on. "A girl must be like a blossom, with honey for just one man. A man must live like a honey bee, and gather all he can," says the King of Siam to Anna.

Hot Sex is "screwing" in the most depersonalized sex-object way. Loren Hardeman does this in classic style, "poised over her, like a giant animal blocking out the light until all she could see was him . . . as he slammed into her with the force of the giant body press she had seen working in his factory on a tour just the day before." Depersonalization is also evidenced in the curiously anonymous heroes and heroines of Victorian pornography, which catalogs lustful ventures with only an occasional first name, circumstance, date, or place, but with a tyrannic monomania for all the details of genital interlocking.

For the Hot Sex male, any playmate will do. Sex is something one does to a female, or—phrased in a slightly more subtle way since the demise of Victorian prudery—sex is something one does for a female. Personal physical pleasure is the prime concern; sensitiveness and responsibility are minor. Hot Sex relationships are casual in their impersonalism. The Roman poet Ovid expressed this nonselective, anyone-will-do approach to sporting when he described Corinna, the lady who sent him into rapture. "It is no single she whose beauty calls forth my passion. No, there are a hundred causes to keep me always in love." Ovid's beloved Corinna was in reality anyone. The modest one, the literary one, the dumb one, the short one, the austere one, the saucy one, the flirtatious one—they all appealed to Ovid's passion. A more recent but more restrained expression of this impersonalism and anonymous aloofness comes through in the poignant, tragic, animal aggression of *Last Tango in Paris.*

Proving one's manhood depends on an imposing list of conquests. In a Hot Sex relationship, one can escape the unbearable burdens of time, change, and aging simply by multiplying experiences. Like the passenger on the train in Marcel Proust's *Remembrance of Things Past,* the Hot Sex male or female darts desperately from one window to the next, from one bed to the next, in hopes of encompassing all sexuality. A Hot Sex society is entropic and self-destructive because it lives by possessing and conquering without investing anything of the self. Its lifeblood is the never-satisfied compulsion to perform, whether this be the pressure on the male to prove himself every chance he gets, or the equally destructive (male-imposed) pressure on the female to satisfy the male ego with the blessing of a mutual orgasm or, better, mutual and multiple orgasms.

Hot Sex attitudes are also typified by the American fascination with what appears to be an unlimited variety of "perfect" sexual techniques, positions, and combinations, all of which must be experienced. Hot Sex is the worried quest for mutual orgasm at all costs, the anxious search for the "perfect" partner or, better still, the "perfect" organ. Hot Sex is embodied in the Freudian debate over the relative merits of clitoral and vaginal orgasms, ignoring the facts of female anatomy and physiology.

With its dualistic roots in the separation of soul and body, male and female, spirit and matter, the concept of Hot Sex has forced our culture to despise the body. Despite all liberal protestations, our society, especially in America, cannot accept bodily contact in any but the most "innocent, asexual" way. Hot Sex is sterile, antiseptic, and antisensual. Unable to accept the female as a person, a Hot Sex culture is equally uneasy with nature and the cosmos. In place of the earthly cosmic myths, the rich cycles of nature, and the diffused sensuality-sexuality that characterize many tribal nomadic cultures, the Hot Sex mentality substitutes the treacherous lure of the Parsifalian quest for the perfect partner with the perfect organ and technique, the love-story myth, and the belief that despite its segregation from life—in fact because of this isolation—Hot Sex, genital sex, is IT.

This fear of the body is also manifested in our obsession with nudity and the naked female figure. Our society generally accepts pictorial female nudity in *Esquire* but exhibits some anxiety when confronted with it in such magazines as *Playboy* and *Penthouse.* It is only reluctantly tolerant of the nakedness of hard-core pornography and X-rated movies. Social nudity is tolerated only when safely fenced in at a resort or camp. Even in the privacy of their own homes, parents are often upset when their children see them naked. Countless marriage counselors have reported the uneasiness of married couples with their own nudity when alone together.

For the female at least, lifelong and sexually exclusive monogamy must be maintained in a Hot Sex culture as *the* sole way of life. Adults are socially safe only when packaged as androgynous couples. We consequently place a wide variety of pressures on young people to compel them into early marriage. Patriarchal monogamy is the inviolable monolith of our economic, political, and social fabric. Where would capitalism be without the patriarchal nuclear family and the aggressive competition of our consumer-object-possession-oriented Hot Sex consciousness?

In our Hot Sex culture, marital fidelity is synonymous with genital exclusivity, and sexual intercourse is equated with intimacy. Consequently, every sexually mature single person poses a threat to the monogamous monolith. The unmarried, widowed, and divorced are assumed to be sex starved because Hot Sex attitudes presume that people cannot be fulfilled without constant genital expression. Intimacy among the unmarried must, according to the hypocrisy of Hot Sex values, be resolved by marriage. The extramarital relation can exist provided it is hidden. Once it enters the light of day, it must end or win out in competition with the existing marriage. Although no statistics are available, we suspect that more often than not the serious extramarital affair culminates in divorce. In contrast with the routine and faded romance of the marriage, the fresh affair, with its flavor of forbidden fruit, certainly has more going for it.

Some popular reports have given the impression that the traditional extramarital affair is undergoing a revolution in the swinger, or mate-swapping, phenomenon. Actually, this is not accurate, for the swinger is as much guided by Hot Sex values as is the cheating spouse. In the traditional affair, socially unacceptable sexual expression and romance are kept in the dark. The swinger modifies this by bringing the physical expression into the open only among members of his subculture. Emotions and personal involvement are forbidden. The swinger allows himself the partial safety valve of sexual variety, but he continues to view any real interpersonal involvement as a threat and potential competition.

■ Early Cool and Hot Sex

These patriarchal, genital, property-oriented, performance-obsessed Hot Sex attitudes have guided human behavior and family relations in our Western world for more than a hundred generations. But traditional patterns have evolved and changed drastically with the years, and we are now in the midst of a conflict of opposing cultures. The 1970's are witnessing the onrush of a new system of values we call Cool Sex. Conflicts always contain a certain fascination, but this one is absorbing because we are participants in projecting the future of male-female relations.

The Cool Sex mentality is older than the Hot Sex system. From what we know today, early man's life was similar to that of the higher primates and some contemporary primitive hunting societies. Such life styles exhibit little specialization of male and female functions, except in the areas of birth and child rearing. These are cultures that have not yet discovered class structures or private property, where men and women relate with a mutuality that places equal value on their economic contributions to the life of the community. Because of their physical prowess, the men are the hunters who bring home meat and skins. But the women are equally important. They work a variety of miracles, transforming seed into corn and raw materials into cooked food, medicines, tools, and clothing. Above all, since few primitive cultures understand the causal relationship between sexual intercourse and pregnancy, it is women alone who are thought to generate the mystery of new life in their wombs.

The economic position of woman in early tribal life was

essential to her position as man's equal. Economic viability and independence for women are key requisites for a Cool Sex system of values. Some anthropologists believe that women were the ones who first discovered the possibility of planting seeds and cultivating crops. From this venture in farming came other economic contributions by women: the first crafts and medicines; the first spun cloth, baskets, and pottery; and the first markets for bartering surplus goods and produce.

Early human consciousness involved a oneness with nature. There was no split between heaven and earth, between matter and spirit. The cosmos was alive with gods; the earth was the womb of all life. In a maternal world all things rise from the earth, so what we label consciousness had its roots in Mother Earth. This Primal Uroborus, as the Jungian historian of psychic symbolism, Eric Neumann, suggests, was not a simple female mirror image of our own patriarchal consciousness. Mother Earth was mysteriously self-fertile. She had phallic powers. She combined both male and female in her unsegmented nature.

Human sexuality was also viewed in this unsegmented way, and placed in the same context as animal sexuality. It was a primal sexual consciousness with a polymorphic character that blended sensuality and sexuality into one. Controls over sexual behavior emerged naturally from the tribal community, resting on tribal and totem taboos that served the community. Typically, in matrilineal societies, there were no double moral standards to guide the social or sexual behavior of men and women. Because property was communal, people were not concerned about paternity or legitimacy of heirs. Family lines were traced through the mother, the source of all life. One eastern Australian tribe, for instance, believes that girls are fashioned by the moon and boys by wood lizards. In Queensland, the thunder god supposedly makes infants from swamp mud and inserts them into the mother's womb. Hunting a particular kind of frog, sitting by the fire or leaping over it, cooking a special kind of fish—all can lead to pregnancy.

The Pueblo Indians thought maidens could be fertilized by a heavy summer shower, while the Celtic Saint Maedoc was allegedly conceived when a star fell into his sleeping mother's mouth. The founder of the Manchu dynasty was conceived by a maiden who ate a pomegranate dropped in her lap by a magpie. Longfellow records Winonah was quickened by a western wind, subsequently giving birth to Hiawatha. In such cultures woman's place was on a par with man's, and the whole community formed a real family. When a man married, he moved in with his wife's tribe, much as the early Hebrew patriarchs did.

Today's Arapesh of New Guinea, the Lepchas of Sikkim, and the peace-loving Pygmies of Africa still have many of these earlier cultural attitudes toward sex. Primary sexual characteristics are a source of merriment and satisfaction. The result is a complete lack of confusion over gender and sexual identity. There is little homosexuality as we know it, no models of male or female, no heroes or martyrs to emulate. Some primitives, interestingly, are not satisfied with this simple and flexible view of male and female. University of California anthropologist Barbara Voorhies has studied five societies that recognize a third gender. Among the Navajo Indians, for example, there is the *nadle*. A Navajo can be born with this gender status, as a hermaphrodite, or select it later in life as an alternative to either the masculine or feminine state. A *nadle* may engage in either male or female work, dress as male or female, serve as a mediator in disputes between men and women, preside at certain religious ceremonies, and marry a spouse of either sex.

Another variation of flexible sexuality has been uncovered by anthropologist Denise O'Brien in at least twenty African societies: a woman can legally marry another woman and assume all the responsibilities and functions of husband and father. In these marriages, the female wife may choose or be assigned male partners who will father children for the female couple, but with no recognition as legal or social fathers. These "woman marriages" are not homosexual marriages. They are based solely on social and economic grounds. In one form of female husband documented by O'Brien, the woman is a surrogate male kinsman, taking the place of a deceased brother or father and serving as father to his children and husband to his widowed wife. In a second type, the woman takes a wife because she wants to. A barren woman may take a wife to prove her social ability as a parent. A woman may also accumulate considerable wealth by marrying other women, both from the payments from men who serve as sexual partners for her wives and from the bride wealth her daughters will bring when they marry. Some working women also find it helpful to have a wife to care for their children and perform domestic chores.

The flexible egalitarian status of men and women began to fade when mankind turned from hunting to farming, and then to creating cities and empires. Men and women were quickly segregated as castes, with men specializing in the more public social functions of king, worker, merchant, warrior, scribe, and other specialized tasks, and women relegated to less specialized and more domestic social duties.

Hot Sex values began emerging in earnest when the ancient empires of Babylon, Assyria, Sumer, and Egypt introduced the concepts of private property, class structure, and the patriarchal hierarchy. These cultures still retained many of their matriarchal traditions. The ancient psychic theme of the Divine Mother continued to provide the framework through which the male ruler received his power and authority. Thus the great pharaohs of Egypt were enthroned on the lap of Queen Isis, the Divine Mother. This theme persists in portraits of the Christ Child reigning from the lap of his mother.

During this era, the male began to assert his dominance. This was probably only an extension of the earlier, subtler sexual segregation in the hunting tribes, which surrounded the female functions of pregnancy, nursing, and menstruation with taboos and rites of purification. The male caste also began defining sexual mores in their own terms, justifying the subjugation of women and the restrictions placed on their sexual behavior with the image of the vagina as a wound or trap threatening man with castration.

A radical shift in sexual attitudes, and the first true expressions of the Hot Sex mentality, appeared around 1000 B.C. This revolution can be traced to two sources: a new consciousness among the Hebrew prophets and a philosophical revolution among the Greeks. Both were based on a male revolt against Mother Nature. Men began to seek mastery over nature, not by worshiping it, but by subjecting it to some higher principle.

For the Hebrews this meant a male god, alone in his supremacy over all creation. Creation could no longer be a natural unfolding and fruition of the primal Matrix. It became the product of a male command from above giving form to the primeval chaos of matter. A chasm opened up between God and the world, between uncreated spirit and created nature. The idea of a transcendent god corresponded with a new social development. The solitary male ruler and the functional segregation of men and women were expressions of the male's growing awareness of himself as master over nature and the feminine. The holy war became the characteristic sacrificial rite of the dominating male caste. Sex was segregated from everyday life and relegated to the home. In the patriarchal religion, everything would descend from the intellectual male god at the top to unformed matter and the female.

In this same era, classical Greek philosophy developed the similar idea of a transcendent spirit that reduces the visible material world to an inferior and dependent position. According to Plato's philosophy, man's intellect originates in a purely spiritual world, aloof from time, space, matter, and change. Somehow this pure intellect falls into the lower world of matter, where it is imprisoned in a body as some sort of test. The soul first takes the form of a male but is gradually cast down even further into the form of a female or lower animal. Women thus become a symbol of bestiality and the lower carnal side of human nature. Salvation can only be achieved when the intellect frees itself of matter and sexuality.

This dualistic Greek philosophy, echoed in the Persian cult of Mithra and combined with the patriarchal religion of the Hebrew prophets, forged the real essence of our Western Hot Sex mentality. Sex was segmented from life. Males dominated society. Women assumed a subordinate role as chattel. And the body, with its emasculating sexuality, became the deadly enemy of rational man.

■ Christian Hot Sex

Countless studies have been made of the denial of human sexuality in the ascetic traditions of early Christianity. Christianity was trapped in the conflict between its patriarchal conception of God, religion, and the male-female relationship on one side and the idealistic equality of all on the other. "Man was not created for woman but woman for man," for "the husband is head of his wife just as Christ is the head of his body the church." But at the same time, "In Christ, there is neither Jew nor Greek, slave nor freeman, male nor female." This conflict was compounded by another tension: that between the Hebrew doctrine of creation, which affirmed the goodness of the body, and the denunciation of the body in Greek Platonic thought. The sexist patriarchal values won out over egalitarianism, just as negative asceticism subdued the holistic view of sex among the early Hebrews.

During the Middle Ages three images of woman prevailed: as virgin, as wife, and as whore. Only as a virgin could a woman hope to gain a position on a par with the male. Somehow, in a very tortured logic, the church fathers conceded that a celibate woman could be converted into a "male" and share in his intellectual and spiritual nature. Unlike the enlightened legislation of the late Roman Empire, Christian doctrine placed married women on a much lower plane than celibates. Married life and sexual relations were tolerated as very much a third-rate way of life compared with celibacy.

"The fear of sexuality," Rosemary Ruether points out, "is the primary experience of self-alienation of the mind from the body. Since male/female relations are the prime social expression of how people view the mind-body relationship, it is only natural that a fear of human sexuality and the rejection of the body will lead to a relationship between men and women that can only be expressed in terms of the male subject [mind] and the female object [body]." This fear ultimately abolishes the possibility of men and women relating to each other with any kind of mutual interpersonal communication mediated by the primal sacrament of the body, sexual union. Thomas Aquinas expressed this tension when he admitted, "I feel that nothing so casts down the manly mind from its heights as the fondling of women and those bodily contacts which belong to the married state." Aquinas pinpoints this unresolved but male-biased tension when he concedes that "a good Christian [male] is found towards one and the same woman to love the creature of God who he desires to be transformed and renewed [as a 'male'], but to hate in her the corruptible and mortal connection, sexual intercourse and all that pertains to her as a wife."

For centuries marriages were alliances made by males to gain certain advantages or protect some interest of the consenting families, tribes, or nations. Such matches were vulnerable to the changing tides of politics and economics. What had once appeared to be an advantageous alliance could easily become a burden to be cast off and replaced by a new, more favorable alliance. Although divorce had become increasingly difficult in the Christian community, a man could always arrange to send his wife off to a higher life as a "spouse of Christ" in some convent and then, "widowed," arrange a new marriage of greater convenience. This pattern of marriage prevailed well into the sixteenth and seventeenth centuries.

Functional marriages, coupled with the growing fear of human sexuality fostered by Christian asceticism, completely overshadowed the ancient Biblical view of the family as the center of God's blessings. In all fairness, we must point out that Christianity only accentuated the ambivalence of Greek and Roman societies toward love, marriage, and sexuality. In earlier times, men and women accepted sex as a natural human appetite. Love and passionate affairs were pastimes. Marriage was an inescapable social duty. All three could be taken separately or jointly with no real conflict among them. Christianity brought the conflicts hidden in this earlier pattern to the surface by placing the three elements in opposition.

The common medieval view of woman was that of the whited sepulcher: outwardly beautiful and desirable, but corrupt and vile beneath. A man might learn to love a woman, but only if she denied her sexuality and became a "male" by chastity. Benedict and Scholastica, and Francis of Assisi and Clare were two religious couples in this tradition; and the seventh-century Saint Audrey and her husband, Egfrid of Northumbria, practiced the celibate, or "brother-sister," marriage advocated by Christians everywhere. To what extent the average Christian followed the example of ascetic Audrey is hard to ascertain, but monasteries abounded everywhere, and the writings of the times are filled with praise for celibate married couples who sought the higher life. What had been with the Romans merely unromantic and lusty became unromantic and dirty—a situation ripe for revolution.

The revolution came with the wandering trouvères of Languedoc. The troubadours were born of the mixed marriage of Christian and Moslem cultures in Spain and southern France. They blended the Arabian love of Platonic philosophy with the Christian Catharist fear of sex and the body. There were several midwives involved in the birth of courtly love: the lusty male-dominated Teutonic values of the Franks, who viewed women as playthings for men's enjoyment; a certain hedonism introduced by Eleanor of Aquitaine; a new interest in and misinterpretation of Ovid's classic poem *The Art of Love,* a Roman textbook on methods of flirting, attracting lovers, and consummating romps in the hay; and, finally, the growing cult of the Virgin Mary.

In *The Allegory of Love,* C. S. Lewis claims that the idea of courtly love embodies one of the three or four major revolutions in human attitudes and values. Its advent was a true social revolution because it completely inverted the traditional positions of men and women, elevating women to a level far above that of mortal men. Courtly love endowed women with the highest feudal rank: lordship. The courtly lover was as much subject to the whims of his beloved lady, who had the power to confer on men the grace of her favors, as the knight was to those of his lord. But, in keeping with customs, love and marriage could not mix. Hence one's beloved was always another man's wife, and the love relationship was viewed as truly Platonic.

The Platonic purity of early courtly love found the practical realities of medieval life difficult companions. Men and women lived a communal life unknown to us. Houses had no hallways between private enclaves of individual rooms, so bedrooms doubled as passages to other chambers. Understandably, sexual intercourse was hard to banish to the privacy it enjoys today. The adult world was everywhere, and children as such did not exist. A short infancy of six or seven years quickly ended when the youth was apprenticed to some tradesman or rich family. Once past the toddler stage, young people were considered merely miniature adults, and treated as such in their exposure to adult sexual behavior.

As the courtly love tradition matured during the Renaissance, romantic love as we know it mingled increasingly with human sexuality, even in the attitudes of the new class of wealthy burghers. By the fourteenth century the consummation of a romantic extramarital relationship in sexual intercourse had gained acceptance in some segments of society. Thus the extramarital affair as we know it today came into being for the first time in human history. Prior to this, adultery usually meant only the bawdy physical coupling of a male with some willing or unwilling married female.

Protestantism carried the revolution of courtly love into a new dimension by fusing the idea of romantic love with marriage. The early reformers rejected the medieval ascetic view of marriage as an inferior way of life for the Christian. They rejected monasticism and at the same time restored the Jewish view of the family as the center of religious life and nurture. They championed the value of conjugal love between husband and wife. But they left intact the traditional patriarchal values that subjugated women to men and defined them gently in terms of their servant roles as mothers and dutiful wives. Courtly love had softened but not eliminated the traditional male-female hierarchy. The Calvinists in particular were too hard-working and righteous to waste time or money on illicit love affairs, so they borrowed the tenderness, idealism, romanticism, and idolization of woman from courtly love for use in their own Christian marriages.

Gradually the structure of the family in Europe and America was transformed, along with the sexual attitudes and values that supported it. This evolution has made the last four centuries a critical prologue to our present conflict of Hot and Cool Sex cultures.

McLuhan and Leonard suggest that in conjunction with the development of movable type and the printing press, the essential tools of hot communications media, human life also became increasingly visual and compartmentalized. Architecture became infatuated with the idea of visual enclosures, private rooms connected by hallways. Bedrooms became ultraprivate domains, no longer to be shared with guests. Childbirth and dressing retreated to the privacy of the bedroom, while children were given the privacy of their own worlds. Sexual activity was hidden from everyday life, taking on an aura of mystery and the forbidden. In Victorian days women hid their legs in billowing petticoats and covered the indecent legs of their furniture with similar garb. With this complete privatization of sex, Hot Sex achieved its ultimate segmentation from the total personality.

The impact of all this was most noticeable in the changing attitudes toward children and their role in the emerging nuclear family. In the traditional European family, and especially among the landed nobility, only the first-born male was important. He would inherit the family's land and wealth, while subsequent male offspring often turned to the church for a living. The daughters were quickly married off for whatever advantage might be gained for the family and heir. Infancy lasted an isolated seven years before the young adults were apprenticed to a trade or to serve the adult community outside the family. The more affluent might send their male offspring to the university at twelve or thirteen. Parents tended to ignore their infant children, for few wanted to risk the emotional trauma of loving a child who had less than a fifty-fifty chance of surviving more than five or ten years. Children were treated as miniature adults, but their presence in the adult world was that of an occasional appendage. The heir was special, but his brothers and sisters were allowed to mingle with their illegitimate siblings and other offspring within the family retinue.

This changed radically with the new middle-class family of the businessman, the industrial worker, the burgher. The first-born son lost some of his primacy and joined his brothers and sisters in the growing privacy of his parents' home. With major advances in the prevention and treatment of childhood diseases and the increasing need for formal education, childhood became a way of life distinct from that of the adult world.

In medieval times no one was concerned when youngsters saw or participated in sexual relations. After all, they had been born with the stain of original sin, and as miniature adults they were only doing what adults normally do. However, in the privacy of smaller families, children entered a new world innocent of sexuality. The privacy of the home became a bastion against the vile outside world in which the mother dutifully protected the purity of her offspring.

With this new attitude toward childhood, the middle-class wife's role also changed. In the past, husband and wife had shared the productive work of the family unit because the male worked at home on the farm or at a cottage industry. By the late nineteenth century, men had to be free for a workday away from home. The increasing privacy of the home thus coincided with three other alienations: the alienation of men from the home, the alienation of wives from their husbands' productive work, and the alienation of homes from industry's competitiveness. For her entire life a mother was expected to devote her full time and energy to the nurture of her children. The ideal Victorian wife was also expected to provide a haven for her husband, bruised by the impersonalism and materialism of the industrial world outside. The patriarchy of the husband and first son prevailed. The denial and repression of sexuality in the Victorian era are well known. But they deserve mention here as prime examples of Hot Sex values in full bloom. The isolation from sex experienced by Victorian children was also imposed on the married woman. Though the mother of many children, she conceived these innocently in her sleep. She was even supposed to be oblivious to her bodily organs and functions. Sexuality was a sign of brute nature. It belonged only to the male.

Like the concepts of Hot and Cool Sex and of the troubadours' courtly love, the Victorian cult of True Womanhood was a cultural myth, real yet unreal. Its reality was its functional role in middle-class society. Its unreality stemmed from the naïve belief that only the middle class existed, or counted. The myth excluded the mass of poor. The working class was stifled to provide support for the middle class's leisure. Within this oppressed working class, no one was more oppressed than the wife or daughter laboring to supplement her husband's or father's wages. Exploited in work, she was exploited even more by the sexually repressed Victorian male when she turned to prostitution in her struggle to survive. Yet this double exploitation only served to confirm the sanctity of the Victorian home and the glories of True Womanhood.

In the Victorian era, Western nations were plunging into an orgy of growth, colonization, and exploitation. Industrialization required the creation of millions of unfeeling, unthinking human cogs. The American frontier required tremendous reserves of aggressive competitive male energies. In *The Transformation: A Guide to the Inevitable Changes in Humankind,* George Leonard may have oversimplified the positive function of Victorian repression, but there is some real truth in his brief sketch:

Sexual anxiety became the chief agent of dis-ease. The most effective (if temporary) remedy for concupiscence is good hard work and plenty of it. Instead of masturbating the young man cuts down another tree. And when he masturbates anyway, the young man works off his guilt, gets out of himself, by cutting down two more.

■ *Graham Crackers*

Contrary to what might be expected, the idea of segmented Hot Sex did not come to America with the Puritans. The Pilgrims brought a much more open and earthy Elizabethan spirit to the Plymouth settlement in 1620. The Pilgrim Fathers may have preached vehemently against the sins of the flesh, but they never classified sexuality as a sickness. Some historians have even suggested that, when it came to sex, the late eighteenth century was probably the most open period in American history. The marriage manuals of that era certainly treated sexual relations as something quite natural, enjoyable, and healthy.

All this reversed suddenly in the 1830's with the advent of "The New Chastity." In 1830 came the Second Great Awakening, the strongest and most influential religious revival to shake America since the days of Jonathan Edwards. The contagious fervor of revivalists like Lyman Beecher, Asahel Nettleton, and Charles Finney turned upper New York State into the "Burnt-over District," with an estimated 100,000 converts a year. This fundamentalist fervor swept over the neighboring states and into the west as several prominent temperance lecturers shifted their concern from liquor to the evils of sexuality and all sensual pleasures. The most popular and influential of these social revivalists was a New York City physician, Sylvester Graham, who pictured the human body as a fortress under siege, with only its five senses standing guard. People, Graham argued, could not live in harmony with the world. At best they might hope to survive for a time by constantly opposing all the threats of a hostile world outside. To gain even a temporary reprieve from inevitable death, Graham urged his followers to block out every awareness of sensation within their bodies. Dreams and fantasies became mild forms of insanity, and any consciousness of a feeling in any organ of your body a sure sign that something was wrong. The healthy person should sense nothing from within. All his attention and energy should be directed against the treacherous forces outside.

Graham naturally concluded that sexual desire and sexual intercourse were the most dangerous threats to human health. He warned that men under thirty were too weak and immature to withstand the trauma of intercourse. Even older men should limit themselves to once a month. For Graham and his mass of followers the consequences of "excessive" sexual activity were unlimited, including as they did:

languor, lassitude, muscular relaxation, general debility and heaviness, depression of spirits, loss of appetite, indigestion, faintness and sinking at the pit of the stomach, increased susceptibilities of the skin and lungs to all atmospheric changes, feebleness of circulation, chilliness, headache, melancholy, hypochondria, hysterics, feebleness of all the senses, impaired vision, loss of sight, weakness of the lungs, nervous cough, pulmonary consumption, disorders of the liver and kidneys, urinary difficulties, disorders of the genital organs, spinal diseases, weakness of the brain, loss of memory, epilepsy, insanity, apoplexy;—abortions, premature births, and extreme feebleness, morbid predispositions, and early death of offspring.

As if this list were not enough, Graham traced the dire effects of copulation to every organ in the body. Sexual activity, he warned, gives the skin "a sickly, pale, shriveled, turbid and cadaverous aspect" along with a thick covering of boils, blisters, and pimples of livid hue. Blood pumped into sex-debilitated lungs by an "over-excited and convulsed heart" may rupture the blood vessels, producing hemorrhages in the lungs and blood gushing from the mouth and nostrils. In *The Transformation,* Leonard quotes Graham's marvelous and terrifying conclusion: "The violent convulsive paroxysms attending the acme of venereal indulgence often cause spasms in the heart . . . sometimes producing aneurisms, or bursting of its walls and suffering the blood to gush out into the pericardium; and causing sudden death in the unclean act."

As a prescription for this horrifying prognosis, Dr. Graham offered a unique remedy. The stomach and digestive system are, he believed, directly and closely tied in with the reproductive system. Hence whatever excites the stomach will also excite the genitals, with gruesome results. "All kinds of stimulating and heating substances, high-seasoned food, rich dishes, the free use of flesh, and even the excess of aliment [food], all . . . increase the concupiscent excitability and sensibility of the genital organs." The remedy included a regimented life with a diet of his bland but organically nutritious graham crackers to quell lusty desires. Graham associations quickly appeared in cities of every size. Boston and New York had their Graham boardinghouses, while college students set up "Graham tables" in their cafeterias and dining halls.

Graham's influence continued long after this death, in 1851. Another physician, Dr. John Harvey Kellogg, added a little variety to this bland diet when he invented cornflakes. Like graham crackers, these were eaten unadulterated by any condiment like sugar or milk that would reduce their passion-sedating effects.

The antisexual hysteria generated in this movement spread everywhere. Respected physicians in Europe and America panicked at the supposed debilitating effects of masturbation. William Acton, a respected diplomatic figure, advised Englishmen to sleep with their hands tied above their heads or behind their backs. For women, physicians commonly recommended locked chastity belts or surgery to remove the clitoris. For men, the recommended treatments included circumcision, insertion of a silver wire through the foreskin, spiked penile rings to discourage erections, blistering the penis with red mercury ointment, cauterizing the spine and genitals, surgical denervation of the penis, and, in extreme cases of uncontrolled masturbation, even removal of the penis and testes.

The impact of Drs. Graham and Kellogg on public health in America was devastating, especially for women. The historian Page Smith cites an informal survey that testifies to an epidemic of nonspecific sickness that swept over middle- and upper-middle-class women in the nineteenth century. Catherine Beecher, the sister of Harriet Beecher Stowe, asked her friends to report on the health of the ten women they knew best. Only two of the two hundred towns thus sampled had a majority of healthy women. "Habitual invalids" and "delicate or diseased" women outnumbered the healthy by anywhere from four to ten times. In her own "immense circle of friends and acquaintances all over the Union," Miss Beecher could not recall "so many as ten married ladies born in this century and country, who are perfectly sound, healthy and vigorous."

Leonard suggests that the Hot Sex Victorian fear of sexual activity and the resulting epidemic of sick married women "was perhaps the only acceptable and efficient birth-control method of the time, as well as being a way of reducing inevitable man-woman pressures [in the privatized home] to an endurable level."

With their wives frequently unavailable for sexual intercourse, Victorian men turned to exploiting lower-class women to satisfy their drives. Writing in the journal *Medical World* at the ebb tide of Victorian repression, Dr. Addison David Hard remarked that four of every five men in New York City suffered from some form of venereal disease.

The intense domestication of women and suppression of sexuality soon filled the Victorian home with tension and contradiction. The inevitable revolt began with Sigmund Freud's rejection of Victorian hypocrisy. At first his flushing of sex out of the Victorian underground threatened all that our civilization held dear and true. The flapper's gyrating dance was viewed as "orgasmic release" vented by females revolting against a society that denied middle-class women any sexual expression.

Through Freud, women began to reclaim their rights as sexual persons. Freud brought sex out into the open, but in so doing he merely made it more intensely Hot Sex, genital sex. The male soon found a way of turning Freud to his continued advantage, of using the sexuality of middle-class women to reinforce the pervading Hot Sex roles even more effectively than Victorian repression had. This occurred, as Rosemary Ruether points out, at the same time that the sexually repressive work culture of earlier capitalism was being transformed into a consumer-oriented society. The erotization of the domestic wife was quickly adopted by the new consumer society as its prime advertising image, to sell products and pacify the male frustrated by the impersonalism of his business world. Thus the Freudian sexual revolt actually added to the segmentation of human sexuality.

McLuhan and Leonard have defined this Hot Sex fragmentation of human life with insight and precision:

Since the Renaissance, it has seemed necessary to pen them [the forces of life] up in separate compartments. The industrial age built more than its share of these boxes. It split class from class, job from job, profession from profession, work from play; divorced the self from the reality and joy of the present moment; fragmented the senses from the emotions, from the intellect; and, perhaps most importantly of all, created highly specialized and standardized males and females.

But without the compartmentalization of the sexes, we probably could not have had the industrial revolution. How many of our technological advances derive from an emphasis on male aggression and the will to dominate nature? How much of our Western culture has depended on or been conditioned by the values, attitudes, and social expectations of the Hot Sex tradition? Could Western science have evolved without the Hot Sex drive to subdue and conquer nature, without the Hot Sex segregation of mind and body?

The basic Hot Sex images of maleness and femaleness remain unchanged. Freud's insights wrought a partially castrated revolution; the Hot Sex culture endures, however weakened it may be. Hot Sex is a stage of consciousness that Western man must pass through. It was and is our adolescence as individuals and as a thinking species.

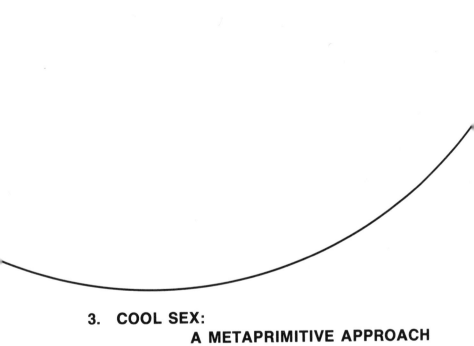

3. COOL SEX:
A METAPRIMITIVE APPROACH

The same neural-hormonal forces that cause an erection can make the sky look bluer.
—MARSHALL MC LUHAN AND GEORGE B. LEONARD, "The Future of Sex"

A society, in short, that is willing to think of itself as changing can find useful, tested patterns of living in the past which can be adapted to new needs.
—ELIZABETH JANEWAY, *Man's World, Woman's Place*

McLuhan and Leonard suggest that the real sexual revolution is taking place today among college students. Obviously there are many changes in attitudes and values prevalent among this generation regarding human sexuality and male-female relations. But in our experience most young men and women in college quickly trade in their easy-going premarital attitudes for a traditional set of values when they contemplate marriage. Pressed on this issue, it turns out that they really accept many of the traditional Hot Sex attitudes of possessiveness, role stereotyping, and romantic love-story myths. Even those who are most vocal and public in their rejection of the traditional institution of marriage and engage in nonmarital cohabitation often subconsciously reaffirm the Hot Sex values and expectations. On several occasions when we have pointed this out in counseling, the reaction has been a very irritated and vehement denial of what any outside observer can easily see.

Still, the common analysis by both professional and lay observers is that today's college generation is the vanguard of our sexual revolution. This appraisal can be supported by two facts. First, the sheer reality of numbers. In 1960 there were only 20 million single men and women in America out of an adult population of 116 million. In 1972 there were 43 million single Americans out of 139 million. The second undeniable fact is that premarital sexual intercourse has nearly run the gamut of Herman Kahn's four levels of social mores, from totally forbidden to public acceptance. Premarital sex was totally forbidden in public opinion before World War II and before the advent of the contraceptive pill. Since then our society has gradually learned to tolerate premarital sex when private and discreet. Today it is not uncommon for college men and women to return home for vacation with a close friend who then shares their bed, much to the consternation of even the most liberal parent. What used to happen in the privacy of the college dorm, off-campus residence, or motel is now surfacing in the home.

In no way are we denying the long-term importance of changing mores among today's youth. Even so, we are convinced that the real revolution in sexual attitudes today is occurring among white middle-class married couples in their thirties and forties who have gained a certain amount of financial independence and leisure.

Financial security and leisure are critical to any exploration of alternate life styles. Black, red, and brown Americans are generally interested in the traditional middle-class American way of life—a wife, several children, two cars, and a suburban home. They are still striving for the American dream many whites have enjoyed for decades.

A central factor contributing to financial independence and leisure has been the return of married women to the economic world after and often before their children are off to nursery school. This is not a revival of the male-support-or-replacement role women held in Biblical or medieval times as manager of the family estates or business for an absent husband. The working wife's role today is outside the home. She has a salary that may be an essential supplement to the husband's wages or may provide those material extras that make a revolution in mores feasible. The economic independence of women is indispensable for any move away from Hot Sex patriarchy.

A second factor tending to place white middle-class couples at the vortex of our revolution is their personal experience of having tried to grow as persons for five, ten, or fifteen years while abiding by the Hot Sex stereotypes, and realizing in the process that something is wrong with the values they originally accepted. Such couples often evolve a strong, essentially healthy bond as a couple that gives them the security necessary for opening up their relationship and exploring something beyond the exclusive togetherness of Victorian romantic exclusivity.

The two central elements in our picture of Cool Sex are the restoration and maturation of male-female relationships to equal partnerships without sex stereotypes and fixed roles, and the overthrowing of the fear-motivated segregation of human sexuality from everyday life, with its consequent reduction to genital interlocking.

In the radically new milieu of a technological, contraceptive society, with its suburban ethos of leisure and pleasure, we are subconsciously creating a new vision of the relationship between men and women. It is a vision of an equal partnership, an open relationship of peers and friends engaged in the lifelong process of maturing as unique sexual persons. We all seem to agree that the grand old stereotypes of American males and females are dead. Today we have no real heroes, and few antiheroes. At best we may have some nostalgic but futile attempts to reincarnate dead heroes. Those individuals who do gain broad appeal are so obviously unique that they only reinforce the Cool Sex message.

We have to accept the fact that times are changing, which means that the development of human nature continues to find new expression in new patterns of human relations. Most of us are willing to admit the outside world is changing, but not many of us are willing to admit we are tied into this changing environment.

Human nature is still engaged in the process of evolution. There is a vital lesson in Paul Klee's statement that "becoming is superior to being." Change—growth—is essential to all life. This is not a comfortable philosophy. It is not easy to live in a culture where masculinity and femininity are no longer eternal archetypes.

■ *Low Definition*

In a Cool Sex culture we create the expressions of human sexuality in our everyday lives, and each unique expression has its own value. When we model ourselves on someone else we limit our potential. Friends may help with their support, but we need to develop the ability to define our goals, the ability to stand alone.

In a Cool Sex culture it is obvious that men can no longer measure their identity as males in terms of aggressiveness, number of females conquered, or male progeny sired. "Join the Marines and Become a Man" is no longer a guarantee of manhood. Today, our cultural values have shifted enough so that we no longer accept a successful career in the armed services as the epitome of masculinity. In the past a woman could find a socially accepted identity in the magical phrases "his wife" or "their mother." Today male and female identities must come from within, from self-actualization.

As traditional concepts of masculinity and femininity change in a Cool Sex culture, marriage and the male-female relationship also take on a diffused, low-definition character. Tolerance of pluralism is characteristic of a Cool Sex culture, but a Cool Sex attitude also requires acceptance of the real possibility of alternate life styles for yourself as well as for others.

All men and women should be free to explore and express their own developing personalities in a culture with a minimum of imperatives beyond the basic rule of not exploiting others, sexually or otherwise.

Rooted in the equality of men and women, a Cool Sex consciousness must be governed by a single moral standard. Its guidelines are not divided into one set applicable to men and another to women, or into one set for one's own

wife and another, looser standard for all other women. Likewise, Cool Sex values are not divided into those governing
the unmarried and others governing married couples.

■   *An Ethic of Knowing*

The prime environmental factors we must consider are our
contraceptive and reproductive technologies.

Until about a hundred years ago Western morality reluctantly tolerated sexual intercourse for the sake of populating
the kingdom of God. Sexual intercourse was not to be enjoyed, particularly by women. In this framework, masturbation, fornication, contraception, and extramarital relations
were all immoral. For the single person, holding hands or a
brief embrace and kiss was the limit of acceptable behavior.
With a marriage license in hand, however, anything became
acceptable provided it ultimately led to procreation. Four
moral codes existed, one for single males, a second for nice
single girls, a third for married men and other men's wives,
and, finally, a special strict code for one's own wife.

What happens, however, when sexual intercourse is rendered nonprocreative on a regular basis? The potential for
conception can now be removed from coitus permanently by
vasectomy and tubal ligations, on a monthly cycle by three
dozen different pills, and individually by diaphragms and
condoms. Today we don't even need sexual intercourse for
reproduction. We can resort to frozen semen, artificial in-
semination, embryo transplants, and, soon, artificial wombs
and asexual cloning. Nonprocreative sexual intercourse obviously raises the serious question of what moral guidelines
we are going to accept for a society that has effectively
turned the vast majority of sexual intercourse into what the
Oneida Community called "amative intercourse."

While self-actualization and personal growth are a prime
concern in a Cool Sex society, each of us also has an in-
tricate and complex network of commitments and responsibilities to other persons. The needs and responsibilities of all

the persons involved in or affected by a relationship must be taken into consideration. Whether one is married or single is not of itself crucial.

A second major consequence of separating sexual intercourse and procreation is that we can once again see sexual intercourse as a way of relating and knowing. In a Cool Sex culture we relate to persons; persons are unique, unmatched, unparalleled, unprecedented, unequaled. If each person is unique, the grounds for competition in human relations are automatically eliminated. Sue may have a sharper mind than Jane or Bill, and Bill a more athletic physique than Tom. But they cannot be compared in a competitive way against a common standard or model. Nor can they be compared against each other, for then we have to cope with an unlimited range of unmeasurable variables. Unique combinations of qualities cannot be weighed in any objective quantitative way. In a Cool Sex society competition in human relations is a total distortion.

■ *Synergism*

Human relations guided by a Cool Sex attitude are synergistic rather than entropic. Cool Sex does not mean the end or the lack of emotions, intense feelings, concern, or warmth. It does mean that relationships should reinforce and strengthen one another rather than compete in a negative way.

As individuals we grow, not in isolation, but by relating in an intimate way to other persons. We help each other grow when we relate as individuals rather than as objects to be acquired. Human relations in a Cool Sex society should be involving and intimate, simultaneously embracing and inclusive rather than closed and exclusive. One whose sexuality is person-oriented will seek to know another person in depth. When this knowing involves genital intercourse it will be in the Biblical sense of *yahdah*, "knowing," rather than in the spirit of pursuing an object to screw and conquer.

In *Motivation and Personality,* Abraham Maslow suggested a theory regarding a "hierarchy of basic needs" in our society. He argues that each of us strives to meet, in sequence, five basic needs for: physiological well-being; safety or security; social and interpersonal gratification; self-esteem and respect; and, finally, self-actualization. In this hierarchy the basic physiological necessities must be satisfied before we can deal with other needs. Art and philosophy are not congenial companions of starvation.

American and European societies have largely solved the problems of meeting our physiological and security requirements. This is not to deny the reality of poverty, but even with this reality there is the conviction that we could meet these needs if we set certain priorities. If, however, the middle class has satisfied its basic physiological and security needs, then our task is to move on to meet our interpersonal needs. Here the central question becomes evident: Can we meet these needs as long as we accept a cultural norm that limits us to a single close and intimate relationship at any one time?

Dan Peterman, a specialist in personality theory at Pennsylvania State University, believes that the "deepest interpersonal needs of which Maslow spoke can only be met fully through the establishment of a number of close relationships that share certain characteristics. No single relationship, no matter how intimate, can possibly fulfill all requirements. On the other hand, numerous relationships, without minimal conditions of trust, openness, mutual commitment, and shared interest, would not suffice either. Consistently meeting basic interpersonal needs over time probably requires formation and maintenance of a number of relationships of very high quality."

Originally Maslow estimated that the average American meets about 50 per cent of his needs for love, interpersonal support, and intimacy. By 1967 he was much more pessimistic: "The truth is the average American does not have a real friend in the world." Even our closest "friendships" often include concerns that cannot be shared, special interests that are not open for mutual exploration. Often, Peterman states, experiences we would like to share with a close friend are taboo because our friend happens to be of the same sex or of the opposite sex, of a different age, married or single, related or unrelated to us. Even though we are blessed with many friends, there are many times when society forbids these friends to really support and complement our needs. In the mirage of plenty, we starve.

The popularity of the sensitivity movement and group encounters is only one of the more visible signs among Americans of dissatisfaction with their isolation and loneliness. The enthusiasm and joy of people in an encounter weekend and their amazement at the new intimate relations they have found are a devastating reflection on the distance and aloofness that prevail among the oldest and closest friends in our culture.

A Hot Sex culture fragments, segregates, and isolates the young from the middle aged and alienates both of these from the old, the married from the single, the male from the female. A Cool Sex culture integrates.

In our mobile, transient society, youth seem to suffer most from the cultural imperative restricting us to a single in-depth relationship at any one time. The young wonder about the risk of investing in a relationship such as marriage when statistics indicate they will likely be disappointed and left hanging with nothing somewhere along the line. A relationship that "feels good" today may not continue to satisfy all one's needs a few years from now. So why commit oneself at all? So long as we maintain our cultural norm, and limit ourselves to only one genuinely close relationship at a time, young and old alike will continue to have this fear, and perhaps rightly so.

A Cool Sex culture could resolve this fear and also provide a much richer ground for personal growth by promoting the radically new ideal that each person should develop several simultaneous close relationships that reinforce one another. This new model would, in Peterman's words, "accept interpersonal needs as naturally being multifaceted, shifting over time, and therefore requiring a new norm emphasizing development of a cluster of intimate relationships." Developing a set of rich relationships, Peterman warns, requires new skills in the initial stage of building a relationship. Cultivating a network of deep interpersonal relations and continuing to develop and maintain a meaningful career and avocational interests require that we dispense with the elaborate ritual games designed to build trust slowly, move rapidly into open, honest communication, and then make decisions about the extent to which we want to invest in a particular relationship. This kind of direct approach also allows one to be more aware of limitations and of why they are different in different relationships.

A Hot Sex male approaches women with a homogeneous mind set that lumps them all into one category of sex object, with a sex orgy as the ultimate experience. The Cool Sex consciousness and morality, with the open integration of sexuality with everyday life, are the opposite of the Hot Sex fantasy of libertine free love. Men or women who accept the challenge of an Open Marriage and Cool Sex values are very selective about relationships they invest time and energy in. Several of our friends and acquaintances have commented on this paradox and the fact that most men, in particular, do not appreciate the Cool Sex moral values underlying human relations on all levels. In *John & Mimi,* an autobiographical account of a free marriage, Mimi Lobell denounces the Hot Sex chauvinists who feel that she or her husband should be ready and anxious to have sex with anyone who comes their way because they both believe in a nonexclusive primary relationship. Another friend shared with us her irritation in these words:

Because I am candid about my belief in open marriage and because my husband writes and lectures on the subject, many men think I will be just delighted to jump into bed with any of them, strangers or not. They feel I should not be "discriminating." When I explain that for me sexual involvement is a continuation of a deep and meaningful relationship, they don't understand. They think I'm just a "big talker with no action." This reaction irritates me, but I've learned to expect and accept it as part of the price I have to pay. It also helped me overcome my own anxiety with this attitude when I saw men quickly justifying their feeling of rejection by calling me "inhibited."

Human energy is a priceless commodity. So is our time on this earth. Why then should we waste them trying to establish relationships that will limit our growth? We can spend our limited energies in a negative social structure, holding on to the one or two in-depth relationships we have struggled to establish in the hope they will last a lifetime and meet all our needs. Or we can use our energy to deepen a variety of relationships: one or two primary long-term relationships, and a changing spectrum of long-, medium-, and short-term satellite relations of varying intimacies. As Peterman suggests, "this investment in good *present* relationships is thus a more dependable basis for a secure future." It also contains a richer potential for individual growth.

■ *Touching*

A Cool Sex mentality diffuses the spotlight from the genitals over the whole body and embraces the full range of our emotions and senses, thus freeing sexual intercourse of its present imperatives.

Cool sexuality is expressed in integrated, holistic behavior that is not disturbed by nudity or scandalized by "immodesty," as Michal was when her husband, King David, flipped his skirt too high while welcoming home the ark of the covenant with joyful dance. Hot Sex revels in "the taboo of the graven image of the groin," says Dr. John Money, director of the Johns Hopkins University Gender Identification Clinic and respected authority on human sexuality. He argues that we have many near-psychotic obsessions with nudity that are unhealthy for ourselves and especially for our children. We have little objection to the public display, in either art or everyday life, of above-the-belt sexual behavior associated with lyrical romantic love—hugging, embracing, kissing, caressing. But when this behavior dips below the belt it becomes "carnal knowledge," something lewd, lascivious, and dirty, to be hidden from the light of day and particularly from our children.

Even when nudity has no direct connection with sexual intercourse, our American culture is uptight. The nude female figure may be widely accepted as a work of art, but it provokes adolescent titters from men of all ages. Topless and bottomless female entertainers experience an amusing array of legal ups and downs around the United States each year. Until recently the nude male was totally taboo because the naked male is endowed with a raw, animalistic sex even though the portrayal may have nothing to do with sexual relations.

Dr. Money is very concerned about the segregation of the sexual in our culture. Children are sheltered from any exposure to sexual relations and birth. Money argues that we must learn how to deal more openly with the reality and visual experience of human sexual organs and intercourse in early childhood. "People are very apprehensive that openness and early childhood education will give license to teen-agers to be promiscuous. But children do not imitate everything they see. They can learn things in terms of concept and context." Perhaps a more open attitude in sexual behavior would help young people integrate their sexuality with the rest of their lives and reduce significantly the horrendous peer-group pressures that push children in their early teens to experiment with sexual intercourse long before they are ready for it.

A Cool Sex mentality should integrate the whole range of human communications, including bodily contacts and intimacies—touching, kissing, nudity, and sensuality—with genital intercourse. In his study of *Intimate Behaviour*, Desmond Morris suggests that bodily contact is the most elemental form of communication, but notes that this form of communication goes into steady decline as we leave the infant stage. The infant says, "Hold me tight." The young child increasingly says, "Put me down," while the adolescent asserts his independence when he states, "Leave me alone; let me be what I must be." Morris sees this as a life cycle in which the security essential to the infant gradually yields to the independence essential for the adult. Then, in what he admits may well be a "cynical over-simplification," he dissects this same cycle later on in our lives. Young lovers, like the infant, say, "Hold me tight." They will even emphasize their new need for security by calling each other "baby." For the first time since infancy, physical intimacies once again become a dominant mode of communication. As in infancy, the body-contact signals weave their magic to form a firm bond of attachment. The growing strength and importance of this bond are evident when the lover's plea "hold me tight" is reinforced with the phrase "and never let me go." But when the pair bond has been established and the lovers have a secure relationship, this second "infancy" ends. The new intimacy cycle moves relentlessly on, copying its earlier sequence. As the enveloping intimacies of courtship and the second infancy begin to weaken, a second true childhood begins, and then the adolescent lover moves toward independence. "Hold me tight" yields to "put me down" and the "leave-me-alone" plea for some privacy in a second puberty. This is a perfectly normal cycle that can be handled if the secure pair bond can avoid the pitfalls of remaining in that initial closed possessive phase. The trouble is that most couples are sorely tempted to remain on that level. They then feel trapped. Their independence of action is threatened. The solution is to decide it was all a mistake. Divorce merely echoes the primary separation we experienced as adolescents. But, if divorce produces a new adolescent, then what is this adolescent doing alone, without a lover? Psychologically, after a divorce, each member of the broken pair feels compelled to seek out a new lover with whom he or she can find the security of infancy. In its extreme, this life cycle can create a vicious circle of divorce and remarriage.

Morris goes on to suggest that some married couples avoid this recycling by augmenting their pair-bond relationship with the new intimacies of sexual experience and the shared intimacies of parenthood. So the cycle is not inevitable. The question we raise, which Morris has not considered at all, is whether a new Cool Sex attitude toward bodily contact and intimacy and a parallel openness to the varied intimacies of multilateral relationships would break this cycle. The acceptance of intimacies on a variety of levels with a variety of persons, we believe, would help break the vicious cycle of marriage-divorce-remarriage, resolve the growing tensions of isolation and impersonalism, and facilitate the formation of long-term, open, and growth-oriented one-to-one relationships.

Obviously there are variations within every culture on the acceptability of bodily contact, and many differences among ethnic groups. Ashley Montagu has commented on these in a recent study, *Touching: The Human Significance of the Skin.* The Germans, with their disciplined patriarchal families, are probably the most uncomfortable with bodily contact. The upper-class Englishmen are close behind. The tradition of the nanny and the conditioning of a very distant relationship between parents and children from birth to death have produced a virtual negative sanction on touching in the English culture. For many people of Anglo-Saxon lineage, public demonstration of affection is vulgar.

At the other pole, people of Jewish descent appear quite comfortable with the body and bodily communications. The same is true of Russians, many nonliterate cultures, and Latin or Mediterranean cultures. Only in these ethnic groups is there an ease that allows men to embrace each other or kiss each other on the cheek on nearly any occasion. Scandinavians stand somewhere in the middle.

Class differences are also important in our changing mores of touching, although they are the opposite of our common assumptions. In general one would think that the higher the social class, the less bodily contact there would be. But in the only study of such class differences, a sociologist found upper-class American mothers much more at ease with touching their children than lower-class mothers. Montagu suggests that despite the small size of this local sample, "it is possible that this finding could be [validly] generalized for the American population as a whole, with exceptions represented by blacks and other 'minority' groups."

■ *Satellites*

Marriage, as the most common intimate relationship today, is the one most directly affected by the shift to a Cool Sex system of values. We are convinced that the one-to-one, male-to-female marriage is here to stay. We are also firmly convinced of the distinct value of long-term commitments and relationships on a one-to-one, male-to-female basis. But the common American myth of romantic exclusive monogamy, which originally developed as an adaptation to an environment that no longer exists, has to yield to a more functional pattern. Our hope is that these open pair bonds will evolve as flexible long-term interactions within the context of today's mobility, increasing life expectancies, earlier retirements, more efficient contraceptives, and the accelerating liberation of women.

In a Cool Sex culture, the vast majority of one-to-one pair bonds will begin with a period of romantic possessive exclusivity. This may well be a psychological necessity. However, once they have satisfied this need, most couples will be forced to face a basic choice: to continue the closed entropic union and risk disillusionment when its unrealistic Hot Sex expectations are not met, and when the needs for intimacy are frustrated in today's mobile family; or to face the tensions and pain of opening up their primary unit and creating a support system with the varied intimacies of an intentionally extended "family." For the majority of couples this decision seems to come after several years of marriage, when the children are off to school for much of the day and the wife is left home to think.

The possibility of a role-free, flexible, open marital relationship is unthinkable in a Hot Sex culture. When carried to its logical depths within a Cool Sex set of values and behavioral patterns, this openness would accept a variety of intimate interactions on all levels for both husband and wife, including genitally expressed relations within the orbit of the primary pair-bond relation. Our conviction is that this type of flexible Open Marriage is far more functional today. We believe firmly that its utility will continue to increase. This, however, does not deny the many demands and risks involved in such a marriage.

Several years ago Rustum and Della Roy, two chemists at Pennsylvania State University with years of experience in marriage counseling, encountered a new type of relationship among couples attending retreats at Kirkridge, in the Pocono Mountains. It was a relationship parallel to the marital one that was openly accepted by husband, wife, and a third party. This relationship unexpectedly complemented and reinforced the bond of the husband and wife and appeared also to work very much for the good of the third party. The two relationships appeared to be synergistic. Yet it was not a group marriage or a traditional triangle. It was almost as if this new form took off in a different direction, with a quite unorthodox and novel psychology as its motive and rationale. To label this new relationship the Roys joined minds with the Reverend William Genné, director of the National Council of Churches' Family Life Bureau, and coined the label *comarital relationship.* The new label has proven very useful in the context of Open Marriages and Cool Sex attitudes.

Three years ago Bob had an opportunity to discuss

some of the limitations inherent in the *comarital* term with John Williamson at Sandstone Retreat. An alternative label was inspired by a shooting star falling out over the Pacific. Why not a satellite relationship? It does not have the marital bias inherent in *comarital*. The term *satellite* is also more direct in highlighting the complementary and secondary nature of the relationship within the context of primary pair bonds. Unlike the term *comarital,* it is not biased in favor of sexual genital expression. In practice, we have ended up using the two terms interchangeably.

The satellite or comarital relation is not simply an acquaintance or traditional close friend, for both of these relationships are hemmed in by the Hot Sex restrictions forbidding persons not married to each other to have any intimate relations. It is a very personal and intimately emotional friendship, transcending the taboos and restrictions placed on the traditional friendship, that may or may not find expression in sexual intercourse.

The satellite relationship becomes possible only when all parties are secure in their own identity and accept the noncompetitive uniqueness of every human. For the married couple there must be a secure and healthy primary bond; for the single person, a basic contentment with his or her life style.

Maslow, the Roys, Peterman, and others have highlighted the changes in our environment that make such relationships functional and even necessary: the complexities of modern life, the varieties of educational backgrounds, and expanding personal expectations. With a fairly circumscribed background, it is easy to find one person who can meet all one's needs.

This expansion of human relations to integrate new modes and expressions of intimacy seems to echo a consciousness that appeared in the earliest Biblical tradition. The Jewish people had no word for sex, or sexual intercourse, as we say, until they borrowed these fragmenting terms from the more philosophical urban thinkers of Persia,

Greece, and Rome. The original Biblical tradition did not speak of the engaging, pleasuring, person-integrating total relationship between a man and woman as "making love" or as genital interlocking. Instead they used the simple, rich word *yahdah,* "knowing." Many people, especially the young, think this is a nice Victorian euphemism. But the real meaning of "knowing" in Hebrew is far richer than anything our Hot Sex Western mentality can imagine.

In his study *Sex in History,* Gordon Rattray Taylor pointed to some unusual indicators of Hot and Cool Sex, particularly within British society. He found that certain eras were male-oriented, or what he calls Patrist, in their attitudes, while others were more female-oriented, or Matrist. The distinction is quite close to our Hot and Cool Sex model, for Taylor sees Patrist cultures as authoritarian and disciplined and Matrist cultures as more spontaneous and freer in sexual mores. Interestingly, Taylor uses English fashions, paintings, and law as indexes of these two cultures.

Clothing styles in a Patrist, or Hot Sex, culture are very distinctly masculine or feminine, with male fashions formal, stiff, and very restrained in both color and texture. The properly dressed Victorian man could never be mistaken for a Victorian lady. The army is a good example of a Patrist subculture, at least in this century, with its formality and reserve in uniforms. Fashions in a Matrist culture, such as the era of Charles II (1660–1685), display an almost unisex style. In reaction to Puritan asceticism, both men and women in the reign of Charles II loved ostentation, evidenced in their elaborate lace collars, broad-brimmed hats with giant plumes, and bright-buckled shoes. The men, of course, had their bulky breeches, and the women their skirts, but they shared the same plush materials, gaudy colors, and gay patterns. Matrist fashions are extravagantly colorful, highly individualistic, and subject to frequent changes in fads.

Taylor extends this distinction to hair styling, with Patrist eras preferring smooth, clean lines and Matrist cultures shaggy, loose styles. In the Matrist era of Charles II, men wore immense chest-length wigs deluged with baroque curls.

Taylor finds the same trends in gardening and painting. The art of Patrist eras tends toward peaceful, tidy scenes— tranquil meadows and ships at anchor, and the neat to-piary gardens of the seventeenth century. Matrist art cele-brates roughness, wildness, brilliant color, thundering water-falls, and tumultuous seascapes. In eighteenth-century painting, for instance, the landscapes are true to nature, asymmetrical, filled with a variety of rotting logs, the un-planned and spontaneous. The contrast between Patrist and Matrist art is the contrast between the discipline of Mi-chelangelo's paintings and the spontaneity of Picasso's line drawings, between the formality of ballroom dancing and the formlessness of rock, between the rigid structure of a fugue and the improvisations of jazz—discipline and planning versus spontaneous movement and untamed impulses.

Taylor also points out that Patrist cultures are greatly concerned about crimes against property, while Matrist cul-tures tend to be more disturbed by crimes against persons and problems of food supplies. The current trend in America and England is to reduce the penalties for "victimless crimes"—crimes against property, crimes that are only violations of sexual mores, and the use of soft drugs.

The following two samples of fiction and history should further clarify our concept of Cool Sex values, attitudes, and expectations.

■ *Grokking*

In 1961 an unusual novel came from the conservative dean of science fiction, the pragmatic agnostic Robert A. Hein-lein. *Stranger in a Strange Land* was largely ignored until it went into paperback edition in March 1968. Since then it has gone through sixteen printings to become a kind of un-derground Bible for today's youth, along with Robert Rim-mer's *Harrad Experiment.* Though many elements undoubtedly contribute to the book's popularity, what stands out is the hero's matter-of-fact assumption that sex is a way of sharing and growing closer to many people, not just one or two.

Heinlein uses satire, humor, and fantasy to tell the story of Valentine Michael Smith, the son of the first humans to land on Mars, who was raised and educated by Martians after his parents' early death. He returns to earth with a later expedition only to be shocked by the genital-obsessed, exclusive, property-oriented attitudes of earthlings. The Martian pattern of male-female relations was communal and multisensual, with no rigid distinction between male and female roles. And what earthlings called carnal knowledge and reduced to genital coupling, Mike views as "growing closer," or "grokking," a kind of demierotic relating and interpersonal knowing in the ancient Hebrew sense.

Mahmoud explained what grokking meant to Mike and the Martians in these words:

"Grok" means "identically equal." The human cliché "This hurts me worse than it does you" has a Martian flavor. The Martians seem to know instinctively what we learned painfully from modern physics, that observer interacts with observed through the process of observation. "Grok" means to understand so thoroughly that the observer becomes a part of the observed—to merge, blend, intermarry, lose identity in group experience. It means almost everything that we mean by religion, philosophy, and science—and it means as little to us [earthlings] as color means to a blind man.

Soon after his return to earth, Mike sets up the Nest, a utopian commune where men and women "share water" in a ritual before they share their hearts and bodies. That Mike's "water brothers" included both men and women is reminiscent of the way the Iranian language lacks the gender-identifying pronouns *he* and *she*. Water brothers swam together in the nude and made love on the waterbeds in their Nest. It was an outrageous subversive life style destined to throw earthlings into an angry panic that eventually forced Mike and his water brothers off the earth.

■ **Maithuna**

A century ago a small group of Americans called the Oneida Community explored a type of grokking. The community began with a few relatives and friends of John Humphrey Noyes in Putney, Vermont, in 1831. Its early growth was painfully slow as its members learned to cope with their own needs for a solid economic base as an industrial-farming community, their own evolving religious structure, and the growing animosity of outsiders. Eventually the community included over three hundred members of staunch fundamentalist Methodist faith. One of their most interesting beliefs was their rejection of monogamous marriage on the basis that its acceptance as the Christian ideal represented "the grand apostasy of Christendom." Monogamy was *egotisme à deux,* a violation of Jesus' command that the saints must love one another equally on this earth.

In the kingdom of heaven [Noyes wrote in the community's "Statement of Principles" in 1846] the institution of marriage which assigns the exclusive possession of one woman to one man, does not exist (Matt. 22:23–30). In the kingdom of heaven, the intimate union of life and interests, which in the world is limited to pairs, extends through the whole body of believers; i.e., complex [group] marriage takes the place of simple (John 17:21). The abolishment of sexual exclusiveness is involved in the love-relation required between all the believers by the express injunction of Christ and the apostles and by the whole tenor of the New Testament. "The new commandment is that we love one another," and that not by pairs, as in the world but *en masse.* The restoration of true relations between the sexes is a matter second in importance only to the reconciliation of man to God.

Noyes became increasingly impatient for the second Great Coming of Christ, and decided that one way to prepare for it would be to practice the complex, group form of marriage that would replace monogamy in the afterlife. This practice, however, posed a serious practical problem. The community's limited finances made it difficult for them to handle large numbers of children. In fact any procreation would have been a burden. Noyes solves the dilemma by drawing a distinction between amative intercourse, which any two members of the community could enjoy, and procreative intercourse, which would be only for those selected by the elders to become parents. The practicalities of this distinction required a simple and effective method of contraception. Noyes turned to the East, and adopted a mode of sexual intercourse, common among the Hindus and Buddhists, known as *maithuna. Maithuna,* or, as the Oneida Community called it, Male Continence, is sexual intercourse without male orgasm or ejaculation. In Aldous Huxley's *Island,* the character Will learns of it from Ranga:

"In a word [Will concludes], it's birth control without contraceptives."

"But that is only the beginning of the story," said Ranga. "*Maithuna* is also something else. Something even more important. . . . What we're born with, what we experience all through infancy is a sexuality that isn't concentrated on the genitals; it's a sexuality diffused through the whole organism. That's the paradise we inherit. But the paradise gets lost as the child grows up. *Maithuna* is the organized attempt to regain that paradise."

In his provocative study of the Americanization of sex, *Nun, Witch, Playmate,* Herbert Richardson claims that *"maithuna* totally transforms the meaning and purpose of the sexual act . . . [by] shifting the purpose of the sexual act from excitation and tension release—a purely private pleasure —to the continued communion, heightened mutual awareness, and shared enjoyment of the partners." Ordinary orgasmic intercourse presupposes and reinforces the genital spotlighting and segmentation of sex in the body. Not that orgasm is wrong or undesirable. But in a Cool Sex consciousness, the goal of sexual union is not orgasm or the release of tension. Its sole goal is that very union, communion, mutual contemplation. In Richardson's words, sexual union in the *maithuna* form becomes "religiosexual contemplation, a way of winning heightened awareness of another and enjoying 'God' in and through him or her."

The general idea of *maithuna* in Tantric Yoga is that sexual love and intercourse can be transformed into a type of worship in which the partners are, for each other, incarnations of the divine. In the Buddhist and Taoist counterpart— since the notion of worship is foreign to them—*maithuna* is more a contemplation of nature in its true state.

The Tantric Yoga form of *maithuna* is essentially a way of transforming and directing our sexual energy. In the Yoga symbolism this is described in terms of directing our sexual energies from the loins to the head. In Yoga, the spinal column becomes a Tree of Life, with its roots in the earth and its branches or flowers in the heavens beneath the firmament of the skull. The base of this Tree is the abode of *kundalini,* the Serpent Power, an image of the divine life energy incarnate in nature and asleep under the illusion of *maya.* Yoga consists in awakening the Serpent and allowing it to ascend the tree to the heavens. At the base of the Tree the Serpent expresses itself in sexual energy; when it reaches the top of the tree it manifests itself as spiritual energy (but not in our dualistic Western sense of the word).

According to the Tantric view, the energy of *kundalini* is aroused but then dissipated in ordinary sexual activity. However, when sexual intercourse is prolonged and the male refrains from orgasm, this energy is diverted into contemplation of the divine incarnate in one's partner. In the classic Yoga position for *maithuna,* the partners sit with their legs crossed, the woman encircling the man's waist with her thighs and her arms around his neck. Such a position makes movement almost impossible, which is the basic point of the classic Tantric Yoga, to allow the sexual energy to follow its own course without being grasped or exploited by the imagination and will. Meanwhile, the mind and senses of the couple remain open to "what is" in their union and the cosmos without trying to give it direction or purpose.

Tantric Yoga's framework is so totally different from what we are accustomed to in the West that it is easy for us to confuse the symbolic language of *kundalini* and the ascent of sexual energies in the body with terms from our Western physiology and body-soul philosophies. There is one point, though, on which the classic *maithuna* is obviously not valid. Adherents of classic Yoga believe that orgasm and the loss of semen weakens the male by reducing his store of energy. However, the Taoist tradition of *maithuna* takes a more realistic and acceptable position, arguing that male orgasm is permissible in *maithuna* and that female orgasm in fact nourishes and strengthens the male force.

The essence of *maithuna* then becomes much more reasonable. The point of ordinary Yoga exercises and Tantric Yoga *maithuna* is not to stop a natural process like breathing, but rather not to grasp and possess them. Sexual contemplative union naturally delays orgasm. But since there is no value in prolonged and motionless intercourse as such, the purpose is to allow the sexual union to become fully spontaneous. Orgasm is spontaneous when it happens of itself and in its own time, and when the whole body moves naturally in response to it. This cannot happen unless one lets go of his or her own ego in contemplation or meditation. Only then can sexual intercourse become, in the words of Alan Watts, "a melting warmth between the partners so that they seem veritably to flow into each other." And this can happen in a union without any essential connection with orgasm. In other words, what might have been only physical lustful coupling in search of personal pleasure becomes the most considerate and tender form of love.

Consider the psychological value of this Cool Sex approach to sexual intercourse in the context of Alfred Kinsey's findings. Kinsey reported that perhaps three-quarters of all American males reach orgasm within two minutes after the initiation of sexual relations, while a considerable number of American males reach climax within less than a minute or even within ten or twenty seconds after penetration. Kinsey's statistics compare favorably with other studies cited by Ford and Beach in the classic *Patterns of Sexual Behavior.* Most animals are very quick in copulating, so the brevity of American intercourse may not be unnatural. Be that as it may, brevity in human love-making is hardly a virtue, especially for the woman and female orgasm.

Contemplative intercourse, in a modified form of *maithuna,* is not love without delight or enjoyment. Rather, it is love that is not contrived or willfully provoked as an escape from the habitual empty feeling of an isolated ego or from the boredom of life. Nor is it a substitute for the polymorphic sensuality of Cool Sex. *Maithuna* has no specific aim—certainly not orgasm, mutual orgasm, or mutual multiple orgasms. Contemplative intercourse is simply a man and woman together exploring their spontaneous feeling and being. In *Nature, Man and Woman,* Alan Watts sums it up when he warns:

It is not quite correct to say that such a relationship goes far beyond the "merely sexual," for it would be better to say that sexual contact irradiates every aspect of the encounter, spreading its warmth into work and conversation outside the bounds of actual "love-making." Sexuality is not a separate compartment of human life; it is a radiance pervading every human relationship, but assuming a particular intensity at certain points. Conversely, we might say that sexuality is a special mode or degree of total intercourse of man and nature.

The *maithuna* of Tantric Yoga and Taoism is then very much in the tradition of Cool Sex: it lifts sexual desire and intercourse out of the limited genital segment and into the totality of personal expression and communion. This means a new sensitivity to the depths and satisfactions of contacts the Hot Sex mentality views as the "preliminaries" to sexual intercourse. It overcomes the orgasm, performance, and technique obsessions of Hot Sex. It becomes fully human. Sexual love in the contemplative spirit provides the conditions under which we can become aware of our mutual interdependence upon other persons and the world, of our oneness. Tantric Yoga and *maithuna* are only secondarily techniques.

The psychic counterpart to the bodily awareness and polymorphic sensual intimacy is the feeling that one can express his thoughts to another just as they are, without the slightest pretense or need to color their essence. At times, the contemplation—the "vibes" and "chemistry"—is such that this psychic union can be experienced without the need to express one's thoughts in words. Such psychic communion is perhaps the rarest and most difficult part of any human relationship. Yet to bare one's being, to unveil the flow of one's thought, can be an even greater sexual intimacy than physical nakedness.

■ *An Eroticized Society*

In *Nun, Witch, Playmate,* Herbert Richardson carries this revolution in sexual attitudes, the shift toward a Cool Sex culture, into the broader context. Having traced the evolution of human sexuality through five stages, Richardson concludes with three long-range tendencies:

First a tendency toward the *moralization of sex.* By this is meant the displacement of instinctual (male) aggression as the fundamental sexual drive by the feeling of voluntary sexual love.

. . . second, a tendency toward *the individualization of men and women.* By this is meant the gradual process of growth in self-understanding whereby men and women come to recognize one another not simply as equals, but as beings containing within themselves the possibility of full identification with the feelings of the other sex.

. . . third, a tendency toward *the eroticization of society*. By this is meant the loosening of sexual feeling from its locus in the genitals of the body and the diffusion of that feeling throughout all human interaction so that even business and political activities will not be impersonal, but friendly and "warm."

This broader social context is vital to our understanding of the revolutionary, apocalyptic impact of the shift from Hot to Cool Sex.

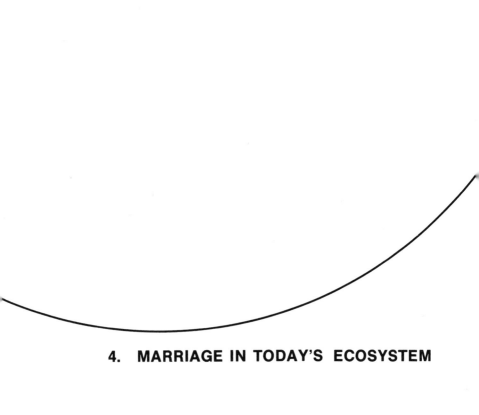

4. MARRIAGE IN TODAY'S ECOSYSTEM

*Faced by rapid social change and the staggering implications of the
scientific revolution, super-industrial man may be forced to experiment
with novel family forms. Innovative minorities can be expected to try
out a colorful variety of family arrangement. They will begin by tinker-
ing with existing forms.*
—ALVIN TOFFLER, *Future Shock*

*Each marriage institution operates within a specific cultural context of
interlocking, interdependent institutions of other kinds—kinship, social,
political and economic. This close intermeshing of institutions means
that as our society is impelled toward change, each institution will tend
to readjust or realign itself in conjunction with the others. Marriage,
because of its very personal nature, has been slower to adapt itself to
change than other institutions; but it, too, must and will change.*
—NENA O'NEILL AND GEORGE O'NEILL, *Open Marriage*

Human behavior is an adaptation and response to our environment. If the environment changes, our behavioral patterns will also change to insure survival.

■ **Life Spans, Etc.**

Over the centuries of our traditional patriarchal pattern of
monogamous marriage, one environmental factor has remained fairly important. Anthropologists estimate that a
million years ago the average human lived eighteen years. At
the dawn of the Christian era the average life expectancy
had risen to about twenty-two years. In the next thousand
years, with improved medical knowledge, it rose to about
thirty-five years, where it stayed until the twentieth century,
when control of contagious diseases and the discovery of
antibiotics rendered a major change. Today the average life
expectancy for female white Americans is seventy-six, for
white males and black females sixty-nine, and for the black
male sixty-one. Within two or three generations the life ex-

pectancy of Europeans and Americans has nearly doubled. In twenty-two years, from 1945 to 1967, the average life expectancy of the newborn Japanese female doubled, from thirty-seven to seventy-three. Medical experts project in the next thirty years an average life expectancy for Europeans and Americans of over 100 years, or even as high as 120. This doubles, triples, or even quadruples the time a man and woman can expect to spend together in the exclusive intimacy of the traditional marriage, barring, of course, other variables, such as divorce.

This single factor of life expectancy becomes even more critical if we use infant mortality in calculating the averages. Including the number of children who die in their first year, we discover that in England in 1550 the high rate of infant mortality brought life expectancy down to eight and a half years, while in Geneva it was four years and nine months.

Infant mortality rates are also an important factor in the changing structure of marriage and the family. The number of children born, the percentage that survive, and the socially desirable size of the family influence the way husbands and wives relate to each other. Philippe Aries has carefully documented the common indifference of most parents to their children until the last century. He notes in *Centuries of Childhood* that parents were reluctant to become emotionally attached to an infant who would probably not survive its first year. Of course, with children apprenticed at seven or eight, the opportunity for parents to love their children was gone almost before they passed the crucial survival test. Around 1800, contagious infections took the lives of one of every five infants in their first year. By 1915 in America infant mortality had been cut in half; nine out of ten children survived their first year. In the 1940's penicillin improved this average to more than ninety-seven out of one hundred. Today more than ninety-eight of every one hundred infants survive their first year.

Centuries ago a woman who lived long enough would have fifteen or twenty children, in hopes that several might reach adulthood. Queen Anne, who ruled England from 1702 to 1714, had thirteen children altogether. All died in early childhood except the Duke of Gloucester, who reached the ripe age of eleven. Infant mortality rates among the poor were two or three times higher. Most women spent all their time being pregnant, nursing, and raising their many offspring.

In colonial America the average family had between ten and twenty children, with families of twenty to thirty not uncommon. In mid-Victorian England the average mother gave birth to six live children. In 1972 the average size of the American family, based on a declining birth rate, was down to 2.01 children per family.

Recent changes in expectations are even more interesting. *U.S. News & World Report* capsulated three sets of surveys dealing with family size as follows:

In 1967, only one wife in a hundred between ages 24 and 28 wanted NO CHILDREN.

In 1972, one wife out of every twenty-five in the same age group wanted NO CHILDREN.

In 1965, one out of ten college students in Stockton, California, wanted NO CHILDREN after marriage.

In 1970, it was one out of four students who wanted NO CHILDREN.

In 1967, 6 per cent of American couples wanted only ONE CHILD.

In 1972, 10 per cent wanted only ONE CHILD.

What is likely to happen to the husband-wife relationship if the average woman of tomorrow has only one child and many have none?

Industrialization has accented the traditional mobility of Americans. Vance Packard reports in *A Nation of Strangers* that our mobility provides some extraordinary stresses for marriage and family. The average American moves fourteen times in his life, compared with five moves for the Japanese. Forty million, one-fifth of all Americans, change addresses at least once a year. Many American cities change more than one-third of their population each year. In one Great Falls, Montana, school, 70 per cent of the students and 30 per cent of the teachers are new residents each year. In the labor field, changes in the length of the workweek and in the age of retirement have already had an impact on marriage. In the late 1700's, journeymen carpenters in Philadelphia worked six days a week, from sunrise to sunset. A workweek of seventy or eighty hours at manual labor left men with little time or energy for family life. By 1890, many American businesses had adopted a ten-hour workday, though the twelve-hour day was not uncommon even as recently as 1923. During World War II, the present standard five-day, forty-hour week took firm root. Today the average workweek is thirty-seven and a half hours. Riva Poor has documented the growing trend in many businesses to a forty-hour, four-day workweek or a thirty-six-hour, three-day workweek. The United Auto Workers has been exploring the advantages of shorter workweeks. One Delphi projection sponsored by the U.S. Department of Labor's Manpower Administration has projected a thirty-two-hour workweek by 1980. In another projection, the National Association of Business Economists has predicted that by 1990 the United States would be able to maintain its present gross national product with a five-hour-per-day, four-day workweek.

The economic trends in retirement are equally interesting as a major change in our ecosystem. A hundred years ago a man worked until he died. Retirement and social security did not exist. Then retirement came at ages seventy, sixty-five, sixty-two, and sixty. Today many corporations are moving to a mandatory retirement age of fifty-five. Twenty years ago nearly half of all men over sixty-five were still working. Today that percentage is down to one-fourth, with a further decline to one-fifth expected by 1980. By 1977 more than half the people of age forty-five are expected to be retired, and some predict a mandatory retirement age of 35 by the year 2000!

The economic position and function of women are also

changing. In 1940, some 17 per cent of all the married women in America held outside jobs. In 1972 the percentage was 42, with 7.2 per cent earning more than their husbands. Many men feel threatened by this trend. As males and husbands, they are not happy that their wives might be placed in contact with other men and enjoy the same kind of moral freedom as men. No one has yet documented a correlation between extramarital relations and employment opportunities, but such a conclusion seems logical. Marriage experts today estimate that 60 per cent of America's married men and one-third of our married women engage in extramarital relations sometime during their married lives.

As the economic functions of the traditional Western family continue to fade, one wonders what impact this may have on marital mores and the dominant position of marriage in our society. In 1960 the U.S. Bureau of the Census reported that 51 per cent of the men and 37 per cent of the women under thirty-five were single. In 1971, the percentage of single men under thirty-five was up to 56 and that of single women to 45. One child out of six in America is in the custody of a single parent.

One last factor in our survey is the legal acceptability of terminating the marriage union. Between 1639 and 1692, only forty-two couples in the colony of Massachusetts were divorced—not even one couple a year. Two centuries later Victorian England was scandalized when over 700 divorces were granted in one year. In America in the same year, 1886, there were 25,000 divorces. In 1920, one divorce was granted for every seven American marriages. In 1940, it was one divorce for every six marriages; in 1960, one divorce for every four; and in 1972, one divorce for every three. In 1973, California granted two divorces for every three marriage licenses issued. With no-fault divorce laws being adopted in many states, the California trend is likely to overtake the whole country.

In brief review, we have nine changes directly affecting marriage and the male-female relationship:

1. Expanded life expectancy
2. Reduced infant mortality
3. Smaller families
4. Increased mobility
5. More leisure, due to shorter workweeks and earlier retirement
6. Greater economic productivity by women outside the home
7. Increased open extramarital activity
8. Increase in single parents and single life
9. Increased ease of divorce

These environmental changes constitute an interesting progression from the technological to the behavioral. Medical technology increases our life expectancy, reduces infant mortality, and gives us effective contraceptives. Result: a behavioral and value change toward smaller families. Industrial technology increases our mobility, gives us more leisure, and returns women to economic productivity. Result: a behavioral and value change expressed in the increasing popularity of the single life and a growing acceptance of sex outside the marital union. Of course, the medical and industrial factors are tied together in a feedback network with the behavioral changes, so it is really dangerous to isolate one from the other.

■ *Modular Marriages*

The most important behavioral change is the increased ease of terminating a marriage. It is by far the easiest and most logical modification we could make in adapting the traditional marriage to the technology of recent decades. For the individual, remarriage allows the emotional security of preserving the protective shell of all but one of the values essential to traditional marriage. Divorce and remarriage change only the until-death-do-us-part expectation, and then more often in reluctant practice than in actual acceptance. Young people, single or just married, often conveniently blot out the statistical odds for the nonsurvival of their union. When reminded that divorce is twice as likely when they marry before the age of twenty-two, they push this aside—the possibility that divorce will touch their marriage is for them simply unthinkable.

The fact is that we no longer practice traditional monogamy. We are not a monogamous culture, and haven't been for some time. Professor Jessie Bernard, the highly respected family sociologist, has bluntly pointed out that Americans and Europeans are much better at polygamy than any of the more primitive cultures of Africa, where polygamy is legal. We have simply legalized polygamy on a serial basis instead of allowing a person to have several spouses at one time.

Alvin Toffler, the author of *Future Shock,* argues that "serial marriage—a pattern of successive temporary marriages—is cut to order for the Age of Transience in which all man's relationships, all his ties with the environment, shrink in duration. It is the natural, the inevitable outgrowth of a social order in which automobiles are rented, [Barbie] dolls traded in, and [paper] dresses discarded after one-time use. It is the mainstream marriage pattern of tomorrow." Time has not been kind to this 1970 prediction of Alvin Toffler. Tomorrow is already today.

Rather than opting for one of the more unorthodox patterns of marriage, such as group marriage, most people take the path of least resistance. They marry with the conventional expectations, try to make it "work," and when the relationship no longer works, they start looking for another partner whose development at that point matches theirs. So long as Hot Sex conditions a marriage, the lifelong expectation is nearly impossible, and a series of spouses is close to inevitable.

The common thread underlying most divorces is the Hot Sex expectation that a spouse must satisfy all needs over a span of several decades. Professor Ray L. Birdwhistell, a family psychiatrist best known for his studies of kinesics, or body language, commented on the roots of this Hot Sex expectation in his study of the model American family, which he traces back to the late nineteenth century. This model contained two main components: the first, the "fantastic" notion that one man and one woman should be responsible for satisfying all of each other's emotional needs; the second, the idea that parents should be responsible for meeting all their children's needs. Birdwhistell uses terms like "cannibalistic," "exotic and impossible," and "fantastic" to describe these two expectations, and rightly so. The ideal is never achieved in life, yet it is a very real social model that turns the home into a cage. "Caging," Birdwhistell suggests, is accomplished by reducing meaningful lateral contacts, especially for the parents. Parents and children exist in a self-enclosed unit. Relationships outside the cage are formal and impersonal, and contribute little, if anything, to personal growth and development. Children are raised in this emotional cage and, when old enough, pushed out to set up their own cages, from the isolated cages of suburban homes and urban condominiums and tenements to the smaller cages of reservations for the aged, our "leisure villages."

This sentimental model presumes an incredible synchronization in the growth of two persons, an impossible and lethal expectation, even in diluted form. Yet it is still with us.

Few newlyweds today, no matter how liberated, willingly accept the fact that they cannot possibly meet all their spouses' needs. Furthermore, most women sense that, while men may encourage their wives and daughters to get an education, they do not really want an intellectually equal wife or a financially independent one.

The cannibalistic exclusivity of the Hot Sex marriage requires two adults to avoid intimate relationships with members of the opposite sex. Intimacy outside the cage is immediately equated with infidelity and threat. The couple then is forced to live a symbiotic life as an inseparable pair sharing everything for decades. Unfortunately this is most conveniently achieved when the wife submerges her personal growth in that of her husband and children. When parallel growth is attempted on an equal basis, the end result is frustration and divorce if the sentimental expectation is maintained. This sentimental exclusivity is tied in with another inflammable expectation, born of the Freudian revolution and the sexual liberation of women. This is the new Hot Sex myth, expressed in books like *The Sensuous Woman / Man / Couple,* which argues that sexual intercourse must always retain the passion and romance of the courtship and honeymoon. Moreover, it should always be at the pitch of an earth-shaking orgasmic high, although in every other area of human behavior we accept average performances. One common result of this is an anxiety when expectations are not met, which not infrequently leads to the assumption that there is something wrong with you and your technique, or more likely with your partner and his or her technique. It must be sexual incompatibility. The Hot Sex compulsion is to look elsewhere for sexual fulfillment, for the lost Eden of courtship and the honeymoon. The result is a typically Hot Sex affair, guilt-ridden and frustrated in a different way.

The central problem in serial monogamy is that it does not come to grips with the serious environmental changes noted earlier. The traditionally defined sex roles, status, expectations, and obligations remain inflexible in a society that is rapidly changing, though there is some tendency for experience to soften rigidity in second and third marriages.

In the early years of a marriage most women are still willing to play the traditional roles. The new wife finds joy in bolstering her husband's ego, scurrying about the new house or apartment. In later years she begins to rebel: "I'm a human being too. What about my ego, my fulfillment, my growth?" The Hot Sex male response typically boils down to the complaint that "she's a ball-breaker, a nag, castrating me every chance she gets." And then, "Who needs that kind of marriage?" Divorce, and for the male a search for a new spouse, some sweet, innocent, very feminine woman.

■ Arrangements

There are other attempts to meet the survival and growth requirements of our ecosystem with a minimum of change. Prime among these are "swinging" and the "arrangement," or consensual adultery, both of which modify the Hot Sex equation of sexual exclusivity with marital fidelity.

Swinging is a complex social phenomenon that came to the surface of American life about fifteen years ago under the label "wife-swapping." The label itself reveals an interesting patriarchal attitude toward the wife as property to be exchanged between males. In the past decade swinging has become a subculture with its own set of values, communication networks, meeting places, rules, and etiquette. Nationwide and concentrated in the city, it still has regional variations adapted to the peculiarities of local environs. Nena and George O'Neill, the authors of *Open Marriage,* have given the following definition of swinging: "relating to others on a sexual basis, either individually, in simple partner exchange, or in a group."

Sociologically, swingers are a sample right out of white middle America. Observers have variously described them as reflecting America's "silent majority," politically to the right, church-oriented, middle class with two or three children, antiblack, anti-male-homosexual, comfortable financially, having high school and some college education, suburban, and urban.

Journalist Patrick McGrady, author of *The Love Doctors,* has pinpointed swinging's essential modification in our marriage pattern by focusing on the elements swingers do not change: "The sex is to be kept hot and varied, the new relationship is (above all else) casual." Swingers make one basic modification in the traditional Hot Sex marriage: they allow their spouses and themselves the freedom to enjoy sexual variety with others, provided there is no emotional involvement. Or more directly, in one of the ten commandments of swinging compiled by Caroline Gordon in *The Beginner's Guide to Group Sex:* "Thou shalt never say 'I love you.' "

Swinging retains the Hot Sex reduction of human sexuality to genital interlocking. Extramarital sex poses a serious threat to the traditional exclusive marriage. But the swinger accepts sexual infidelity by modifying his usual definition of marriage with a "selective permeability." Swinging becomes a means of improving the flagging sexual relations within marriage. It becomes a school for learning by observing and participating with other students who are equally concerned, supposedly, with improving their own conjugal sexuality. Infidelity then shifts its focus away from the genitals to the emotional and romantic interpersonal relationship. Swingers don't date outside group situations. They often limit their swings with a particular couple to three or four contacts, lest they get to know them too well. About half of the natives studied by the O'Neills in a swinging subcultural group of the Manhattan Island tribe maintained an active social life with other swingers in and around their territory. The other half kept swinging completely separate from their regular social life.

Typical of the Hot Sex tradition, swinging is highly structured. In *The Beginner's Guide to Group Sex,* Caroline Gordon gives straightforward advice on how to decorate your home for a swinger party, what to serve, what to wear, and how to get it started.

Alex Comfort suggests that swinging may mark the beginning of the end of proprietary sexual attitudes, and prove valuable to a society adapting to sexuality in a zero-population-growth environment. From the reports now available, it seems that swinging will do little else to change other Hot Sex values and attitudes.

Consensual adultery, or an arrangement, is a less structured way of adapting the traditional marriage to the new ecosystem demands. A growing number of married couples permit each other complete sexual liberty on condition that the affair not be brought home. They may have suspicion or even indirect knowledge of what is going on, but as long as they don't have to face it openly, there is no pressure to play the expected social role of the cuckold husband or betrayed wife. Not infrequently consensual adultery includes the additional segmentation of the swinger that there be no emotional involvement in the outside relationships. The adaptation of the arrangement, however, provides only a minor safety valve. The expectation is that this adaptation will reduce monotony and improve conjugal relations, which it apparently often does, while leaving intact all the other Hot Sex attitudes and values of the marriage.

Reliable statistics on swinging and marriages with arrangements are, of course, impossible to come by, but all the indications are that both are becoming more and more common in America as well as in Europe. It may well be that they are setting the stage for our society's informal institutionalization of adultery as an acceptable modification of mainstream marital patterns.

■ Open Marriage

At the other end of the spectrum from the exclusive property-oriented patriarchal marriage is a social model best labeled Open Marriage. Psychologist Herbert Otto has suggested "New Marriage" as a model in which the marital union's primary function is a framework for developing the partners' personal potentials. Abraham Maslow has written of a "eupsychian society," where all relationships are oriented to the growth of the individual person. Psychologist Sidney M. Jourard, in *The Transparent Self,* suggests a type of "serial polygamy to the same person," a marriage in which the participants constantly reinvent themselves and their relationship. Della and Rustum Roy, pioneer analysts of the current evolution of marriage, have suggested we are entering an era of "situational monogamy" wherein traditional monogamy is still upheld as the ideal but a variety of modifications are acceptable in specific situations. With considerable indebtedness to the Roys, we have talked of flexible monogamy as a model. Robert Rimmer's novel *Thursday, My Love* goes still further in suggesting synergamy, a social and religious institutionalized form of extramarital relations that complements and reinforces an open, or flexible, marriage. Our reasons for settling on Open Marriage range from practical considerations to academic honesty. The O'Neills' book *Open Marriage,* which sold 250,000 copies and was translated into fourteen languages, is academically by far the most thorough and practical portrait of the new form of marriage. Hence we will use Open Marriage as our working label and integrate into the O'Neills' description our own insights and comments.

The most essential thing to remember about Open Marriage is its low definition. As a pattern of human relations, an Open Marriage puts flesh on Cool Sex attitudes and values. Open Marriages are therefore custom made and highly individual. There is no single unchanging archetype, such as we outlined for the Closed Marriage. This basic low definition of Open Marriage is reinforced by the fact that each unique Open Marriage is itself constantly growing and evolving. What may have been an Open Marriage can be quietly transformed into the unchanging pattern of a modified Closed Marriage. It would be comforting if sometime in life we could say we have arrived and can now rest. Unfortunately it seems to be characteristic of human psychology that once we have arrived, both the journey and the goal seem to lose most of their meaning and value. Becoming is essential to any definition of human.

Open Marriage, as we see it, is above all else an honest relationship between two people who accept each other as persons, a relationship of two friends committed to an intimate partnership that is nonmanipulative and nonexploitative. The partners share equal status and function. Neither partner is locked into a stereotyped role provided by society.

All the tasks associated with the relationship—domestic chores, financial support, and child rearing—are shared on the basis of convenience, interest, and talent rather than in terms of some predetermined role. The couple accept the fact that they cannot be all things to each other. Each partner therefore has interests and friends that the other may or may not share.

According to the O'Neills, Open Marriages are flexible, unique, and constantly changing, but they are not without some dynamic structure and common characteristics. However flexible these may be, they can still save us from having to decide everything for ourselves.

■ *Living for Now with Realistic Expectations*

"An overriding obsession with the future is a hallmark of the closed marriage," according to the O'Neills. The couple are constantly planning for the future, for their children, for a home in the suburbs, for a second car, for a summer home. An Open Marriage puts all these down as goals secondary to the present relationship of husband and wife. Today, with most Western countries developing their own social-security systems to provide for the retired, sick, and aged, and with the number of children per family drastically reduced, the child-focused, security-obsessed marriage becomes nonfunctional for the middle and upper classes of our society.

The "Now Generation" is not just a catch phrase. Instant communications media and the affluence of many people today have helped create a generation that lives without past or future. Today's youth are notorious for their lack of interest in the past. They are also known for their impatience with tomorrow's promised land. It's "Peace Now," "Love Now," "Equality Now," "Justice Now." In their lack of consciousness of time, today's youth are typically tribal, living in the present. Dehumanizing as future-obsessed society and marriage can be, they also have certain definite advantages. Discipline, order, and willingness to sacrifice present satisfactions for future goals made our great works of art and science possible. One wonders about the impact of a "Now" philosophy on human relations and human creativity. In the long run, we will have to settle for a combination of the two extremes. At this time we seem to be at the apogee of the spontaneous now.

If this swing in time consciousness wakes us up to the unrealistic expectations of the Closed Marriage, something very worthwhile will have been accomplished. The O'Neills give a long list of the unrealistic expectations, unreasonable ideals, and mythological beliefs of Closed Marriage: Marriage should last forever. It means total commitment, belonging to another, never being lonely, never wanting to be with anyone else. It means a relationship in which sex and love constantly improve if you find the right technique. Marriage without children and parenthood is incomplete. Changes come gradually and simultaneously for both husband and wife, without pain or disruption. It means roles for both based on biological design. Jealousy in marriage is a sign of caring. And, finally, your spouse can and will fulfill all your needs—economic, physical, sexual, intellectual, and emotional.

The ecosystem has changed, however, and in the process it has revealed the frustrating lack of realism in these expectations. On the other hand, are the expectations and nowness of the Open Marriage any more realistic? Is it wrong to plan for the future, to sacrifice now to accomplish a long-range goal? Obviously not. In the realistic expectations of an Open Marriage, the O'Neills include the following items: You can expect to share most but not all things with your spouse. Each of you will change, sometimes with considerable pain and conflict. Each of you will stand on your own two feet as a responsible adult. You cannot fulfill all your mate's needs and should not feel guilty over this. Each of you can expect to have different needs, capacities, values, and dreams, because you are different persons. Your relationship as two adults is primary, and children are a responsibility you accept if you so choose. Your relationship, not some outside goal, is the main reason for your being together. Finally, as a couple you can expect growth in friendship and love to continue, because of your mutual open respect and communication.

Privacy: Experiments in communal living, from the medieval monasteries to today's communes and group marriages, have proven the need for privacy. We need personal space. We need to be alone occasionally, to think, to get to know ourselves, to be ourselves, to recuperate, and to relax. Kahlil Gibran put it simply: "Let there be spaces in your togetherness."

In the last decades of the nineteenth century, the togetherness mystique was developed as a counterbalance to the increasing mobility and freedom of our lives. But this safeguard has become a cannibalistic trap preventing personal growth and turning husband and wife into self-destructive parasites. The need for privacy, the freedom to be alone without spouse or children, must be recognized.

Open communications: Birdwhistell's research on kinesics, or body language, has disclosed that as much as 70 per cent of the information exchanged between people is communicated in nonverbal forms. Tribal cultures, which accept the body as integral to the person, are open to and aware of this form of communication. The diffused sensuality due to the lack of taboos on body contact in many tribal cultures is only one aspect of this openness. One of the most devastating results of our taboos against touching is encountered by marriage counselors who deal with the trauma of young people faced with the complete taboo against bodily communication before marriage and the total about-face after marriage. We certainly hope that our youth's consciousness of their bodies and their diffused sensuality will change this.

Communication, like any other relational art, requires skill and facility. But if we are conscious of the context in which we are trying to communicate, sensitive to the right time and mode, our communications will become a productive feedback network that will enrich our own personality and contribute to the growth of others'. This mutual enrichment will include fantasy sharing and even productive fighting on occasion.

Role flexibility: The Open Marriage thrives on the lack of fixed stereotyped roles for either husband or wife. This does not mean that Open Marriage has no roles at all. One cannot exist in a social situation without some roles. The critical questions are how we view these roles, how flexible they are, and whether any of them are sexist. We are not questioning the fact that there are definite, if flexible, biological differences between men and women, but let's not accept the socially created and maladaptive mystiques surrounding what masculinity and femininity are or should be.

Open companionship: An Open Marriage allows both husband and wife to have common friends as well as friends they do not share. However, the married couple should be agreed on the primacy of their own commitment to each other; their friends should be equally aware of that commitment. Setting out clear boundaries gives the couple their identity. But once they are sure of their commitment, they must open up their relationship and relax its boundaries. Otherwise their relationship becomes an impregnable cage as its walls rise higher and higher in self-defense. Openness demands a maturity that does not see a spouse's friend as a threat or competition.

Equality: In Open Marriage, this does not mean identity with one's spouse or a fifty-fifty division of everything, but, rather, respect for the unique integrity of one's partner, a mutual sharing and collaboration.

Identity: This is probably the crucial factor limiting the number of people able to handle an Open Marriage relationship. Open Marriage does require a fair amount of personal identity, self-actualization, and maturity. Partners in a Closed Marriage can lean on each other and achieve a crippled stability from their weaknesses. It may be tenuous and shaky, but it frequently works. In an Open Marriage this dependence does not work because an Open Marriage cannot exist unless both partners are secure in their personal identities.

Trust: This is the basis of the Hot Sex Closed Marriage, just as it is the basis for an Open Marriage. However, the O'Neills distinguish between static and open trust. Static trust is based on the clearly defined expectations of the traditional marriage and on the assumption that we can count on our partners' meeting those expectations. With many of those expectations impossibly unrealistic, the static trust has settled for appearances. Static trust is not necessarily honest, nor does it promote intimacy, communication, and change in the marriage relationship. Open trust, on the other hand, encourages growth in both partners. Its mutuality and candor go far beyond dependability in terms of specific expectations. The O'Neills quote a friend:

Trust is the feeling that no matter what you do or say you are not going to be criticized—it is an open policy of not having to keep embarrassing secrets, and the willingness to say what is in your mind knowing that the other person isn't going to use it against you later on. This is trusting *in* someone, not just trusting him. We can be naked in the presence of the other not just physically but in a real intimacy of thoughts and feelings. The idea is that we know we are not perfect, but we also know that we are not going to be faulted for what we are.

Trust is at once the most necessary component in an Open Marriage and the most threatening. It has to be built into a relationship slowly, unconsciously.

In a number of situations, the mere mention of the word *trust* triggers a very emotional question of marital fidelity and sexual exclusivity, the prime Hot Sex fascination-obsession. In an Open Marriage there is undeniably the possibility of friendships evolving into the intimacy of sexual relations. But even the way we have stated this possibility throws the situation into all the negative stereotypes of Hot Sex values. That single statement ignores all we have said earlier about equality, identity, open companionship, privacy, and recognition of growth needs.

Closely tied in with the concept of trust are the complex questions of sexual exclusivity, fidelity, jealousy, and possessiveness, and the possibility of comarital or satellite relationships, which may or may not involve sexual expression. These questions are critical because they must be faced emotionally as well as intellectually before we can feel comfortable with Cool Sex and Open Marriage as a distinct and desirable way of life.

Of course, both Closed and Open Marriages have their own unique systems of rewards and punishments. Both have their distinct advantages and disadvantages. The Closed Marriage was functional and served the particular needs of a particular generation and social structure. However, that social structure no longer exists. Closed Marriage cannot operate as smoothly and efficiently as it once did; those who try to maintain it will find it increasingly difficult to do so without the support of a living ecosystem.

5.   HOT AND COOL: CLOSED AND OPEN

The new sexuality leads eventually to the creation of a family as wide as all mankind, that can weep together, laugh together and share the common ecstasy.

—GEORGE B. LEONARD, "Why We Need a New Sexuality"

Until you recognize that society is a psychological machine which moulds you without your being aware of it, you are wearing blinkers which make it impossible for you to assess where society is or where it should go in any rational manner.

—GORDON RATTRAY TAYLOR, *Rethink: A Paraprimitive Solution*

When we first began to explore the possibilities of understanding our present cultural revolution, the McLuhan-Leonard distinction between Hot and Cool Sex intrigued us, but so did several other models and theories. It was only after *Eve's New Rib* was published in mid-1972 that we took a second and more careful look at this model. Our contact with the members of the Sandstone Community in California gave us an added incentive as we tried to understand their perplexing experiences and seemingly novel system of values.

A second invaluable aid in our model building has been the positive feedback from guest lectures at colleges and universities around the country.

By this time, you may well be wondering why this concern about paradigms and models. Why not just go ahead and live? Why get so tied up in intellectual abstractions? Why can't you just do your thing and let the pieces fall where they may? Our answer to this is that usually, when people just go ahead and live, the pieces fall on their heads. We desperately need the attraction and lure of some definite future, an ideal, a goal as yet unrealized. Once we gain an appreciation of the thrust of the past and the pull of the future, we have someplace to go, something to do that builds rather than wanders aimlessly.

In his critical analysis of the crisis in American society,

IMAGES AND MODELS   (86

The Image of the Future, Fred Polak predicts some very dark days ahead. If a culture's image of the future is weak or pessimistic, then that culture, Polak maintains, will run into serious difficulties. It will not be able to maintain itself for any extended time. Today, Western civilization seems to be experiencing a total absence of positive, generally accepted images of the future. There are no utopian or eschatological visions. We don't even want to think about tomorrow. Time and life are contracted into the momentary present.

The solution is to develop a new consciousness of the dynamics of time—past, present, and future flowing, staggering toward something new, something, we hope, better, more humane. It is this recapturing of the dimension of time that we find nicely contained in the Hot and Cool Sex myths. They can be very functional because they capture what many people sense intuitively, because they give meaning to the present by clarifying where we have been, because they give meaning to the future by endowing it with the humane and the positive.

In this context we would like to tie together in brief tabular form the paradigms of Hot and Cool Sex with those offered by the O'Neills in *Open Marriage.*

HOT SEX	COOL SEX
Definitions	
High definition	Low definition
Reduction to genital sex	Sexuality coextensive with personality
Genitally focused feelings	Diffused sensuality/sexuality
Time and place arrangements	Spontaneous
Highly structured with many games	Lightly structured with few games
Clear sex-role stereotypes	Little, if any, role stereotyping
Many strong imperatives from socially imposed roles	Few imperatives, self-actualization encouraged

Value Systems

Patriarchal	Egalitarian
Male domination by aggression, female passivity	Equal partnership as friends
Double moral standard	Single moral standard

Behavioral Structures

Property-oriented	Person-oriented
Closed possessiveness	Open inclusiveness
Casual, impersonal	Involved, intimate
Physical sex segregated from life, emotions, and responsibility	Sex integrated in whole framework of life
Nonhomogenous, grossly selective of playmate	Homogenous, finely selective in all relations
Screwing sex objects for conquest	"Knowing" sexual persons
Genital hedonism	Sex as communication

Concerns

Orgasm-obsessed	Engaging, pleasuring communication
Performance pressures obligatory	Sexual relations not primary, truly optional
Fidelity = sexual exclusivity	Fidelity = commitment and responsibility
Extramarital relations an escape	Comarital relations a growth reinforcement
Fear of emotions and senses	Embracing of emotions and senses
Nudity a taboo	Group nudity optional
Sexuality feared, tenuously situated	Sexuality accepted, securely situated
Entropic, property can be used up	Synergistic, mutually reinforcing relations
Frequent alcohol and drug usage	Few drug-altered states
Territory, preservation of social distance	Grokking

In their closing chapter, "Synergy: Couple Power Through Person Power," Nena O'Neill and George O'Neill also include a brief list contrasting the characteristics of Closed and Open Marriages from an anthropological, psychosocial viewpoint. We have taken the liberty of breaking their list up into the four subdivisions just used, to emphasize the important similarities between this set of marital models and our own.

CLOSED MARRIAGE	OPEN MARRIAGE
Definitions	
Static framework	Dynamic framework
Threatened by change	Adaptable to change
Rigid role prescriptions	Flexibility in roles
Calculating	Spontaneous
Value Systems	
Unequal status	Equality of stature
Selfhood subjugated to couplehood	Personal identity
Bondage*	Freedom*
Behavioral Structures	
Locked together, closed in on one another	Open to each other
Limited potential	Infinite potential
Smothering togetherness	Privacy for self-growth
Possession of the other	Individual autonomy
Shuts out others*—exclusivity limits growth	Incorporates others*—grows through companionship with others
Bondage*	Freedom*
A closed, self-limiting energy system*	An open, expanding energy system*

Concerns

Deception and game playing	Honesty and truth
Limited love	Open love
Conditional and static trust	Open trust
Shuts out others*	Incorporates others*
Inhibitive, degenerative	Creative, expanding
Subtractive	Additive
Closed, self-limiting energy system*	Open, expanding energy system*

* Some characteristics in the O'Neill list have been repeated under two of our categories here because they overlap our divisions.

Intriguing as the similarities between our own social model and those detailed by the O'Neills are, the two paradigms become even more informative when compared with a British model proposed by Gordon Rattray Taylor. In *Rethink: A Paraprimitive Solution,* Taylor explores the pendulum swings of societies over the years between cultures that are predominantly matriarchal and those primarily patriarchal in their attitudes and values. In contrasting the permissive societies of late-eighteenth-century England and America with the repressive authoritarianism of the Victorian era, and the repressive Middle Ages with the Renaissance that followed it, Taylor borrows his perspective from Freudian psychoanalysis and cultural anthropology. Instead of the distinction between hot and cool or closed and open, Taylor uses the categories Patrist and Matrist, mentioned earlier.

Social models, however useful and necessary, have their limitations and dangers. If they are stereotypes, they can easily become the tyrannic depressants of personal growth. The inflexible Patrist model looks to the past for its validity. Its validity has already been proven. All the individual has to do is conform. The same is true of Hot Sex and Closed Marriage social models.

PATRISM	MATRISM
Restrictive, especially sex	Permissive, especially sex
Authoritarian	Democratic
Hierarchies	Egalitarian
Women: Low status	Women: High status
Conservative	Adaptable
Looks to the past	Looks to the present or future
Pessimistic, depressive	Optimistic, euphoric
Self-control valued	Spontaneity valued
Homosexuality taboo	Incest taboo
Sexual jealousy	Lack of jealousy
Sky-father religion	Earth-mother or pantheist religion

The high definition of the hot and closed models, or mystiques, makes them easily communicable. Their precision and clarity can often mold human behavior without people realizing that they have themselves subconsciously accepted such conditioning. The Americans who created the myth of the "feminine mystique" were not aware that they were creating a social model. But they did create an extremely effective Hot Sex myth that guided American women, gave them a certain comfort when they conformed, and satisfied the male ego.

However, a simple analysis of the Hot Sex model results in something of a caricature. Some may see in this composite caricature evidence of the invalidity of our analysis. That is unfortunate, but perhaps inevitable, since people feel threatened when confronted by the fact that they have been unconsciously controlled. Once the initial irritation is over, it becomes evident that, however grotesque and damning the Hot Sex model, it is nevertheless very real as a molder of our behavior. This composite is distorted only if all its details are applied to a single individual. No one person could be entirely conditioned by Hot Sex values without becoming a social monster, even though he might live in a predominantly Hot Sex culture. Hot Sex is one extreme of the pendulum's arc, and we are unique composites of hot and cool, living, if married, an evolving relationship that is partially open and partially closed.

Cool Sex, Open Marriage, and Matrist attitudes are not nearly as easy to define as their counterparts. Also, in a culture that is still predominantly Hot Sex, it is practically impossible to describe a Cool Sex situation without having it interpreted in Hot Sex terms. This is a problem the O'Neills have faced repeatedly on television when asked to define Open Marriage. And it is the same problem we face in describing Sandstone, an experimental community in California that has tried to create a transitional environment in which people may experience a Cool Sex culture. The reality of Sandstone or Cool Sex or Open Marriage cannot be described. It must be experienced, picked up intuitively.

Another problem with the Cool Sex model is that it is still evolving. The Hot Sex romantic marriage is weakening as an effective myth. It is slowly being rejected. In the process, a new myth is being created, a new pattern to guide human behavior. The difference is that the Cool Sex consciousness is an unreal composite drawn from certain real elements in various tribal cultures—Marquesan Islanders, Samoans, Hindus, North American Indians—and including some details we cannot document in any society today.

If we are indeed a prefigurative culture, and moving painfully into a new social structure, the role of social models, myths, images, and ideals becomes ever more critical. This role stresses the functional and creative security-insecurity of "flexible and dynamic working models," suggested by Ludwig von Bertalanffy, originator of system-theory analysis and a computer pioneer. As an embryologist, von Bertalanffy understood and appreciated the developmental processes in a growing fetus inside the womb. The embryo is not a preformed human pattern that unfolds totally independently of its environment. A model cannot be set up once and for all; to function, it must be flexible and change in response to input from individual persons, the pioneering minority as well as the more conservative majority. It must be a working model, a guide and not a mold. It should offer insights from past human experience and from the idealism of the utopian dreamer. But it must not coerce. It must leave each individual free to evolve and adapt those elements from the models that best serve his unique needs.

Models should also reduce what Toffler calls "decisional overload." In a culture torn by the acceleration of apocalyptic changes, we are forced to make fast decisions. At the same time, evaluating the pros and cons of each change means spending more time gathering facts to insure the right decisions. But we cannot afford time. We have to act and act fast. If one must choose between the traditional marriage and celibacy, one "informational bit," one switch in the computer, has to be thrown either on or off. Today we have a dozen or more patterns of life to choose from.

Decisional overstimulation perhaps best defines our prefigurative culture. Single life? Celibate or noncelibate? Cohabitation? In a commune? Alone? Married life? Open or closed? Serial monogamy? Divorced and unremarried? Divorced and remarried? A gay union? A triangle? A group marriage? Parenthood? How many children and when? Traditional sex roles or flexibility? And what kind of flexibility? Single parenthood by choice? What kind of changing Open Marriage? The more choices we make, the more time we need. But we don't have the time. Anxiety takes over and, in the end, decisional paralysis.

Unless, of course, we look to flexible, dynamic working models for inspiration and guidance. This is the function we see for our mythic models of Hot and Cool Sex. The printed word may not be the ideal medium for communicating the dynamic realism of Cool Sex and Open Marriage, but we desperately need it to increase the efficiency of our decisions as we face all the varied ways of male-female relating.

PART TWO

JEALOUSY AND FIDELITY

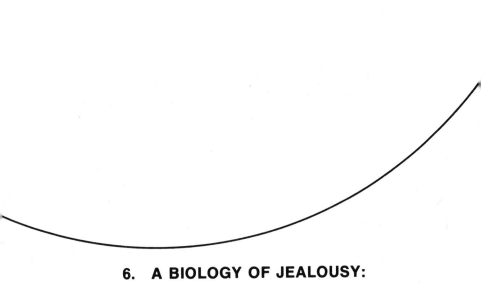

**6. A BIOLOGY OF JEALOUSY:
VARIETY VS. TERRITORY?**

Jealousy characterizes the relationship in which one seeks more power than love. It occurs when the person has not been able to build up enough self-esteem, enough sense of his own power, his own "right to live."
—ROLLO MAY, *Power and Innocence*

Once rid of [the mythology of all-or-none involvement, our society] might find that the relation present in purely recreational or social sex is a uniquely effective tool in breaking down personal separateness–of which the proprietary notion of love is an offshoot–so that, for us as for many primitives, social sex comes to express and cement the equivalent of kinship through a general intimacy and non-defensiveness, reinforced by the very strong reward of realising the suppressed needs for variety and for acceptance.
—ALEX COMFORT, "Sexuality in a Zero Growth Society"

One day in the 1920's the thirtieth President of the United States, Calvin Coolidge, visited a farm outside Washington with his wife. The First Lady, the story goes, gently chided the President about the amorous enthusiasm and energies of one of the bulls, suggesting that it would be delightful if her husband were half as energetic. In reply, Mr. Coolidge, an astute observer of nature, was said to have called his wife's attention to the fact that her idolized bull seldom visited the same cow twice.

In the years since, psychologists and animal behavioralists have wondered about the scientific validity of the "Coolidge effect." In 1952, Jerome Grunt and William Young, two professors at the University of Kansas School of Medicine, confirmed the invigorating influence of a novel sex partner in laboratory experiments. Male guinea pigs, they found, usually rest at least an hour after mating. But if the partner is removed and a new female introduced, the male recovers much more quickly. However, if the original partner is taken out and then returned, the male remains passive. The Coolidge effect has since been documented in a wide variety of animals—mice, rats, guinea pigs, dairy bulls, water buffaloes, sheep, swine, boars, and cats—for both males and females. On the other hand, the eagle and zebra finch, for instance, have very strong exclusive pair bonds. The finch mate for life and virtually never quarrel. The male finch's eye never seems to roam.

The variety of mating arrangements in nature almost matches the number of species. In many fish and birds, a single male will fertilize and incubate the eggs of several females. In other species, the male is very jealous of his nest and allows only his lifelong mate near it. The patas monkeys of northern Uganda are polygamous, but they are possessive of females only when the female is in the male's own territory. On the other hand, the male of the once sacred monkey of Egypt, the hamadryas, never takes his eyes off his harem. If a female wanders a scant ten feet away, the male takes off after her, viciously reminding her where she belongs with a bite on the neck. Male rats will mate with any receptive female, but they make no attempt to monopolize the female as do the territorial-minded seals. In higher animals the most common pattern of mating seems to be an open type of polygamy with pair bonding frequent. Male horses, zebras, asses, pigs, hippos, camels, deer, buffaloes, cattle, sheep, goats, antelopes, sperm whales, and most primate males will repeatedly mate with different females. This polygamous pattern holds even for the chimpanzees and baboons, among which pair bonding and simple family-type relationships are common.

■ Variety and Novelty

Some moralists and biologists have argued that the evolution to pair bonding in the animal kingdom constitutes a moral imperative for exclusive monogamy among humans. In 1954, the Supreme Criminal Court of the Federal Republic of Germany summed up this argument by declaring that there is an objective moral law that "places monogamy and the family before man as an obligatory way of life and makes them the foundation of life for all nations and states." Popular as this enlightened moral position may be, it is in conflict with the findings of cultural anthropology. Anthropologist Clellan Ford and psychologist Frank Beach have produced a cross-cultural study of marriage patterns in 185 contemporary cultures. Eighty-four per cent of these cultures allow men to have more than one mate, though economic factors produce a predominance of one-to-one pair bonding. Less than 16 per cent restrict marriage to one mate, and of these only 5 per cent completely disapprove of both premarital and extramarital relations. More significantly, 72 of the 185 cultures actually approve of specific types of extramarital relations. In most of these, women are more restricted than men. Even so, 10 per cent place no restriction whatsoever on extramarital relations for women, and 40 per cent, according to Kinsey, allow it with special persons such as a brother-in-law or an honored guest on some special occasion, such as a festival or even the wedding night.

Some sociologists and moralists see in our own pattern of lifelong monogamy the ideal form of marriage. But this is hardly a straight-line evolution, for some of the most "primitive" peoples are as strictly monogamous as we are. Moreover, monogamy is not always correlated with other criteria of more civilized cultures. The only over-all conclusion is that most human beings, and the vast majority of cultures, have felt most comfortable with patterns of male-female relations somewhere between the two extremes of sexual promiscuity and exclusive monogamy.

Is this overwhelming tendency toward an open type of pair bonding a functional adaptation to some human analogy of the Coolidge effect? This is a provocative and risky question, but we think the answer may well be yes. The statistics on caged monkeys and married people would indicate so. Both tend to have frequent intercourse with their partners at first, but the passage of time produces a near-celibate relationship. Young couples have intercourse about five times a week. At fifty this is down to about once a week. Kinsey noted an "astonishingly constant rate" of decrease in all sexual activity with age. Married men commonly worry about being impotent as they grow older, but frequently find that a novel female restores their youthful vigor and desire. More than three-quarters of the 6,000 American males interviewed by Kinsey in the late 1940's reported a desire for extramarital relations. Two-thirds of America's married men and at least one-third of its married women have had extramarital relations.

Roger Johnson, a psychologist at Ramapo College and author of *Aggression in Man and Animals,* has suggested a possible application of the Coolidge effect in the use of surrogate partners in marital therapy. The use of surrogate partners was pioneered and then discarded by Dr. William Masters and Virginia Johnson at the Masters and Johnson Research Foundation in St. Louis. Surrogate partners, or "wives," were used as part of the treatment for male impotence. Treatment begins with counseling and psychotherapy, and at the proper time the patient is introduced to his surrogate wife. During this time the patient does not have sexual activity with his wife. Sexual activity with the surrogate partner is carefully guided to allow intercourse only when the patient seems capable of having and maintaining an erection. Among the varied factors contributing to the success of this treatment, we would like to suggest the interplay of novelty provided by the surrogate partner reinforced with the pseudo novelty created by abstinence for a month or two from one's spouse.

This drive toward novelty may also play a role in the taboo against incest. The universal human taboo against sexual relations between parent and offspring, often reinforced with a taboo against sex between other close-blood relatives, serves many social functions. It helps reduce sexual rivalries within the family to a minimum. It strengthens the integrity and effectiveness of the nuclear family group, and also provides support for the pair bond by encouraging alliances with other families through marriage. These positive effects have prompted some sociologists to use the term *exogamy* instead of *incest taboo.*

Exogamy, the tendency to seek sexual and marital partners outside one's own group, may have an interesting psychological basis related to the drive for novelty. In the children's house of an Israeli kibbutz, boys and girls are raised together. They eat together, play the same games, compete, co-operate, and absorb the same philosophy of life. At night they even share the dormitory. The system is designed with the hope that as the children grow up they will find their mates within their own kibbutz and raise children to expand the oasis their parents began. The sociological "law of propinquity," which says that we usually find our mate near where we live, is generally true, but it does not work in the kibbutz. Here, as Lionel Tiger and Robin Fox point out in *The Imperial Animal,* a type of antibond comes into play. In one study of children raised in three major Israeli kibbutz federations, not one couple out of a subsequent 2,769 marriages had spent their first five years together in the same infants' house. Tiger and Fox trace this to the obvious theory that one kind of bond, that of children in a peer group of friends, seems to preclude the emergence, between the group's original members, of a new form of bond, that of marital friendship and sexual relationship. But could it also be that the familiarity of being raised together reduces or hinders the emergence of sexual attraction, which in part seems to depend on novelty?

The results of a sociological study of marriages in two Pakistani villages are similar to those obtained in the kibbutzim. The villages were carefully picked because they were identical in every way except one. Both had the custom of arranging child marriages for their newborn. In one village, the infant bride remains with her parents until after puberty; in the other, the bride goes to her husband's home, where she is raised with him from infancy. The contrast in adult married life clearly shows that being raised with the spouse creates tremendous psychological barriers to a happy married life; most of the couples find it difficult to relate to each other sexually. The researchers trace this to the familiarity of being raised together. Again, we can ask whether the factor of novelty might come into play here, along with other undeniable and more obvious influences.

■ *Personal Space*

If there is indeed a human variant of the Coolidge effect, then what causes human jealousy? Many books have been written in the past twenty years documenting the existence of a "territorial imperative" and its correlation with aggression. These studies have ranged from the pioneering work of Konrad Lorenz, the author of *On Aggression,* and his students, especially Irenaus Eibl-Eibesfeldt and Wolfgang Wickler, through the interpretations of Lionel Tiger and Robin Fox in *The Imperial Animal,* the popularizations of Desmond Morris' *Naked Ape* and *Human Zoo,* to the vulgarizations of Robert Ardrey's *African Genesis* and *Territorial Imperative.*

In the animal kingdom, territorial behavior and conflicts resulting from a desire to defend one's own turf appear widespread but by no means universal. Most of the primates do not defend specific territories. Some, like the howler monkey, will defend the space they happen to be in, but seem unconcerned about a specific turf. Though the two animals are closely related, Thomson's gazelle is vigorously territorial, while Grant's gazelle is not. Some animals are territorial only when mating, some only when nesting, and others only when feeding. Some animals combine two of these types of territorial concern, while others demonstrate all three. All in all, the territorial imperative varies greatly among animals that evidence it. This alone would make any speculation on a human analogy risky.

Yet, as psychologist Roger Johnson has admitted, "the

importance and pervasiveness of territorial behavior in animal societies has provided an irresistible temptation for speculation as to whether some forms of human social behavior, and particularly aggressive behavior, might be manifestations of the same underlying process." Most human societies are based on private property. We labor to acquire it, protect it with laws, and hand it on jealously to heirs. We even tend to become attached to our childhood home, ethnic group, political party, alma mater, favorite team, or TV program, though in a very generalized sense of "territory" or "personal space." However, admitting the existence of a human concern for personal space is not the same as arguing that this is an instinct primarily responsible for human aggression. Furthermore, aggression itself is not the problem; the problem is exaggerated and uncontrolled aggression. Some aggression, some spirit of rivalry, some drive to succeed, and some self-assertion are necessary for both society and the individual.

Aggression, or agonistic behavior, is also very much a part of the courtship and mating behavior of many animals. Most animals are far more aggressive during the mating season, probably due to the increase in the secretion of testosterone, the male hormone, which experiments have repeatedly shown produces aggressive behavior. The males of most species are larger and more aggressive than the females. Females of many species can be housed together, but not so the males. Rats do not fight much until puberty, when the testes begin producing testosterone in large quantities. If immature rats are injected with testosterone, they quickly start to fight. If castrated, they become as docile and peaceful as the females. Tests on a variety of animals in mixed company and alone with other males indicate that the presence of females usually doubles the number of fights between males.

Courtship and mating not only cause aggressive behavior; they also closely resemble it. The male Siamese fighting fish, for instance, uses the same colorful display of fins and gills to threaten invading males and attract female mates. The songs of male birds not only attract passing females, but also mark out territory in which other males will be challenged.

The robin and other birds mark their territory by song, but many of the higher animals, especially those mammals with a well-developed sense of smell, use scents to mark their turf. Special glands strategically located on the cheeks, ribs, and groin secrete simple but very potent substances called pheromones, which rub off or are deliberately rubbed onto brush and plants at the edge of the territory. Rabbits, for instance, create a central burrow with many interconnecting paths radiating out to the encircling path on the boundary. As they patrol the boundaries, their pheromones rub off on the ground and plants, where they serve as a warning that the warren is occupied. The rabbits also carefully deposit piles of feces at key positions. These markers are reinforced by pheromones from an anal scent gland.

The importance of pheromones becomes apparent when they are removed. As long as the territory is well marked and the rabbit stays inside its boundary, it is happy and secure. When it ventures outside its marked turf, it immediately appears tense and nervous, ready for attack by some enemy. The effect of pheromone removal on mice is interesting. In one experiment, mice that had been very aggressive were sprayed with Dior perfume. When put together again and allowed to fight, few were so inclined. Mice deliberately trained to be aggressive were allowed to attack a male sprayed with a male deodorant, Man Power, and another male sprayed with a nondeodorizer. Man Power killed the aggression. The same aggression-trained males were then matched with normal females and females sprayed with Pristeen, a feminine-hygiene deodorant. The fighters attacked both sets of females with about the same intensity, but they were more sexually attracted by the nondeodorized females.

This information may seem unrelated to proving a biological basis for jealousy. Yet there is growing data in favor

of considering this possibility. Clear evidence of pheromones has been found in monkeys. Harvard psychologist
Martha McClintock has suggested that human pheromones
may have a prime role in synchronizing the menstrual cycles
of women living in close association in college dormitories.
And though humans appear to rely very little on their sense
of smell, the efficiency of pheromones is such that they may
well affect our behavior without our being conscious of their
influence.

We know that there are differences between the sexes in
body odors. Women are far more sensitive to odor than men.
They also have about 75 per cent more apocrine glands in
their skin than men. These tiny glands are similar to sweat
glands, but their secretions contain a higher proportion of
solids. Apocrine glands seem to be concentrated in the arm-
pits and around the genitals, where hair tufts serve as traps.
Like the moths that can smell their mates a mile or more
downwind, humans, it is claimed, can detect the presence of
pheromones, especially those based on musk, even when
they are diluted to one part in eight million parts of air.

There is a possibility, mentioned by Alex Comfort in his
paper "The Likelihood of Human Pheromones," written for
the British journal *Nature,* that the human use of pheromones may be limited to childhood. Some psychoanalysts
have suggested the possibility and documented some evidence of a child's being attracted by the opposite-sex pheromone of one parent and repelled by the same-sex pheromone of the other, thus raising speculations about a
biological basis for the Oedipal complex. We also know that
before puberty children have a strong preference for sweet
and fruit odors, with sexual maturity bringing a dramatic
shift in preference in favor of flowery, oily, and musky odors.
Again, the shift is much stronger in women than in men.

Comfort suggests the existence of a male-to-male
pheromone effect that causes either aggression or submis-
sion between men. Is it possible that our new-found enthusiasm for mass-produced and mass-marketed synthetic male

pheromones is now reducing the level of male-to-male aggression as well as the level of male jealousy over females, as it did in the experiments with deodorized mice? At this point it is worth recalling several basic facts about the human brain. First, the limbic system and the paleocortex, the oldest part of our brain, control our basic behavior: survival, mating, hunger, and sleep. Second, according to John Money, this region of the brain plays a major role in male behavior by mediating the assertion of dominance, "possibly in association with the assertion of exploratory and territorial rights." Third, neuroanatomist Paul MacLean points out that this limbic system is believed to have originally been primarily an olfactory brain. The human limbic system seems to combine both visual and olfactory information to trigger both aggressive dominance and courtship-mating behavior. This combined effect could be vital in understanding a possible biological basis for jealousy, for, as MacLean notes, "in primitive cultures in different parts of the world the territorial aggressive implications of genital display are illustrated by houseguards—stone monuments showing an erect phallus—used to mark territorial boundaries. It is as though a visual, urogenital symbol is used as a substitute [or subliminal reinforcement] for olfactory, urinary territorial markings of animals, such as the dog with a well-developed sense of smell."

These are suggestions and questions, certainly not answers. A lot of research will have to be done before they can be resolved. What we are suggesting, with clear and appropriate caution, is that the jealousy demanded by traditional marriage may very well result in part from viewing one's partner as property threatened by loss or as territory being violated. Aggression and threats are the best defense; W. Etkin and D. G. Freedman have suggested that being cuckolded may be the most frequent cause of murder around the world.

This can be tied in with the tensions monogamy creates when confronted with the Coolidge effect. Monogamy's "permanent togetherness," according to Gerhard Neubeck, "results in quantitative and qualitative exposure that may lead to satiation." Habituation can easily dull the sharpness of sexual attraction. Sexual variety, as studies of swingers clearly indicate, can reverse this tendency to lose sexual interest in one's spouse. Novelty can restore the sexual interest within a long-term marriage, but it may also trigger jealousy and the instinct to defend one's territory, or personal space, of which a spouse is part.

Like the O'Neills, "we would like to lay to rest the idea that sexual jealousy is natural, instinctive and inevitable." But we also will stand by our belief that it is related to some biologically rooted behavioral drives. Carl Rogers, a distinguished psychoanalyst and author of *Becoming Partners*, comes closest to our suggestion when he admits, "Indeed, I wonder whether jealousy is something simply conditioned by the culture, or [whether it] actually has a basic biological foundation, like territoriality?"

■ Jealousy

Whatever its biological basis, or lack of it, jealousy is definitely primarily the result of cultural conditioning. There are several cultures in which the concepts of male-female relations and love entail only a minimum of jealousy: the Eskimos, the Lobi of West Africa, the Siriono of Bolivia, and the natives of the Marquesas Islands. In other cultures, such as the Toda of India, jealousy apparently does not exist at all.

Jealousy, according to Gordon Taylor, is a characteristic feature of Patrist cultures, which sanction this emotion and the "crimes of passion" that go with it. Italian opera abounds with this patriarchal theme, and French culture still accepts the revenge of the cuckold husband. In Matrist cultures, Taylor argues, jealousy tends to disappear. The cuckold husband may experience a variety of emotions—irritation, disappointment, even a sense of rejection—but not jealousy. The absence of jealousy is closely tied in with a

particular view of adult emotions and male-female relations.
Anthropologist Wilmon Menard commented on this in his
most recent report on the Marquesan natives: "I have never
found, in the many years that I have voyaged through the
islands of Polynesia, an instance where a native woman fell
deeply in love with her lover. She just doesn't seem to have
the emotional depth, or the capacity to become seriously involved in permanent attachments with a lover."

The casualness with which Polynesian women approach
the male-female relationship may seem shallow or promiscuous. Their lack of possessiveness and jealousy stems from
the way they are raised. In Tahiti and the Marquesas Islands,
children are so idolized that from their earliest days they are
passed around among relatives, loved by all. Sometimes an
infant will spend weeks or months with relatives at the other
end of the island. Loved by everyone, the child soon learns
not to expect a permanent home or to form a strong attachment for one person. He loves everyone, but not with the
exclusive emotion we know from being raised in the nuclear
family. A child whose prime source of affection is his parents
will naturally be very possessive in his responses as an adult.
The Marquesan *vahine* are carefree, flexible, and impulsive
in their sexual behavior because their emotional responses
have been thinned out to the point where jealousy is unknown. This diffusion of emotion has created a culture
where rape and prostitution are totally unknown.

In the Marquesan and Tahitian languages there is no
word that expresses a romantic or spiritual relationship between a man and woman; they merely say, *"Here vau ia-oe,"*
meaning "I want to copulate with you." Menard recalls once
mentioning that in America a man's or woman's heart could
be "broken" by unrequited love or a shattered romance.
"This news convulsed the villagers with hysterical laughter.
They just could not fathom what the heart, brain, or soul had
to do with *titoi* ('joining bodies'). They understood affection
in their mature years only by the sensation centered in their
loins."

This totally carefree approach to human relations has some definite advantages for those who are subjected to the rending emotions faced by an American or European child who loses a parent, or the adult who loses his spouse. But this attitude also has some disadvantages in that it deprives those raised with it of the richness of what we know as adult love.

The Samoans, Tahitians, and Marquesans have a Cool Sex culture, but it is deficient in two essential characteristics. First, the relationship of adult men and women is reduced to "joining bodies." Sexual relations become obligatory rather than optional. Second, Cool Sex should be involved and intimate in a person-related way, and express fidelity between two adults as mutual commitment and responsibility for each other's growth.

Jealousy in our Western culture is deeply rooted in possession. It breeds on insecurity and infantile dependence. The more dependent we are, the more insecure we are; the more insecure, the more threatened by the loss of what we possess. It is a vicious circle, as Abraham Maslow suggests, in which jealousy "practically always breeds further rejection and deeper insecurity." Jealousy destroys the one we love by smothering him or her with demands for exclusivity, and in the process we also destroy ourselves.

The jealous possessiveness of monogamy also has some roots in the rise of capitalism. In an essay in *Renovating Marriage,* John McMurty suggests that "if we take the history of Western society as a data base, the more thorough-going and developed the private property formation is, the more total the sexual ownership prescribed by the marriage institution." Sexually exclusive monogamy, as McMurty views it, "is an institution which is indispensable to the persistence of the capitalistic order." If we reduce jealousy and possessiveness in marriage, what might be the consequences for our emphasis on private property in other areas of our lives?

Jealousy, Rollo May wrote, "characterizes the relationship in which one seeks more power than love. It occurs when the person has not been able to build up enough self-esteem, enough sense of his own power, his own 'right to live.' " Jealousy is an infantile emotion that should decrease as we become more mature, self-motivated, and self-actualizing. One can definitely be involved, committed, and emotionally intimate with a person without being possessive and jealous.

In *The Biology of the Ten Commandments,* Wolfgang Wickler argues that possessiveness and jealousy literally prevent us from knowing another person. It is a great advantage if an individual can be observed against as many different backgrounds and compared with as many other individuals as possible. Enclosing or isolating a fellow man or woman or keeping that person exclusively for oneself and away from others means that he or she will never be fully known in the Biblical sense, or recognized or known again in the biological sense as a partner. In the animal kingdom, the strongest bonds are not found among pairs in which the male treats his mate as a physical possession. More often, the strongest bonds occur among wandering troops or pairs that are faithful to a common territory or meeting place, allowing their partners freedom to associate with other adults of both sexes.

Our growing frustrations with the depersonalizing ownership and jealousy of the Closed Marriage have resulted in a much stronger sense of the social character of sexual relationships than we have had in the past. Alex Comfort suggests that once we get rid of the mythologies of the all-or-nothing emotional relationship and possessive love, we may find that what we view negatively as promiscuity, recreational or social sex, may in fact be "a uniquely effective tool in breaking down personal separateness."

■ *Today's Experience*

What happens to those of us who have been nurtured and fed on the Hot Sex myth as our culture moves toward the more open concept of Cool Sex relations? How do we adapt if we have always believed that jealousy is essential to true love, and fidelity is equated with sexual exclusivity?

The answers can come only from people who have experienced the adjustment. We asked friends and acquaintances for their insights into the problem of handling jealousy in an open relationship. The results of our inquiries have provided some consistent themes.

Bob and Dianne, who wrote to us from England, tried to adjust to an Open Marriage without going through a few years of traditional exclusivity. After five years they have apparently succeeded and now have a strong primary relationship. But Bob admits that adjusting was at times "sheer hell." How did he handle it?

By being jealous, and insecure, and tense! And coming to accept these realities. *By yelling out my anger—loudly and violently.* By becoming more and more aware of my own energy, ability, solidity, independence and self-responsibility.

John Williamson, of Sandstone, was a little more philosophical about his adjustment, paraphrasing a Biblical psalm:

Yea, though I walked through the valley of the shadow of death,
I did fear no evil,
For I knew in my vision,
I was one tough mother . . .

It is practically impossible to put into words the emotion and pain most people experience in adjusting to an open relationship. One couple in their mid-twenties and married for five years gradually came to accept a sexually nonexclusive relationship. The wife summed up her coping with the admission that

at first I kept things to myself, for I felt guilty for wanting someone else, especially when my marriage wasn't lacking anything. I was able to discuss it only after my husband and I became more aware of changing ideas and concepts of marriage. Talking and discussing helped us relieve many tensions, insecurities, and jealousies that might be looming if we had both been silent.

Her husband's views echoed this need for communication:

It would be untrue to say I have no emotional tensions in my shift from an exclusive to a nonexclusive relationship. Twenty-odd years of negative indoctrination is difficult to overcome in two years. However, my wife and I have found that we are very much alike in our wants and needs. *Talking* with each other has been the key to accepting and welcoming sexual nonexclusivity in our relationship. We both know about each other's outside activities, sexual and otherwise. It takes special people to relate to one another as we do. I am not sure I know what the required ingredient is, but maybe it *is* love.

In general, women, and especially women in their twenties, seem to find it much easier than men to adjust to a nonexclusive relationship. One woman just out of college explained to us the tensions she experienced in handling a

sexually nonexclusive relationship with a married man. We enjoy our friends-lovers thing without threat to any other relationship either of us has. [I also have] a sexually nonexclusive relationship with a fellow I lived with for two years. This continues as a strong bond, but seeking nothing save the friendship of deep knowing. I am not living with him now.

It was extremely difficult for me to come to the realization that my lover could love me just as much and still make love with another woman. It took several things: 1) Trust—and I put all my trust in him. 2) Trying it myself and finding that I really could love more than one person at a time without decreasing the love quality for either. 3) Getting to know one of the "other women" quite well to a point of discovering that she was really human and not a witch, etc. 4) A lot of talking, yelling, screaming, crying, and hurt, all of which was not wasted. I like to hear about my men's other women. I know I'm not being compared or rated. They pose no threat to me.

Another single woman in a nonexclusive relationship reinforces and adds to this over-all picture of adjustment her own insights:

In the beginning of my relationship it was hard to adjust to the realization that my partner may not always be involved with just me. But during this time I realized myself that I should not stop him from associating with other women; nor should he stop me from associating with other men. It would be very unfair so soon in our lives for both of us to put such restrictions on each other's actions. We had both realized that each of us needed to have an easy-going bond in our relationship. Having a nonexclusive relationship I believe brought us closer together. We were able to figure things out for ourselves and then able also to share together the experiences. Our relationship is nonexclusive, and still means very much to both of us.

John and Mimi Lobell have written a candid account of their experiences in adapting to a nonpossessive marriage, entitled *John & Mimi: A Free Marriage.* Well done in an overly popular way, it offers insights on jealousy:

Since we have been having sex with other people, I have been jealous only once. I came home one evening after John had been fucking Joanne for the first time to find him beaming, obviously enthusiastic about what had happened. "She fucks like a bobcat!" he exclaimed. I felt threatened. I thought, "Well, he wouldn't say I fuck like a bobcat, but it must be a pretty good way to be, judging from his reaction."

He went on to tell me more, how intense she was,

how it was like a wrestling match just holding her down and so on. John never makes me feel that I am being compared to someone else, which is why I am so seldom jealous, but after this description, I began to suspect that my own responses might not be as intense as they could be. For a couple of days, I talked about how we might make special efforts to elicit maximum responses from me, do a little lab work on me, so to speak. John said it wasn't necessary. "You're fine the way you are." Still, I couldn't help doubting myself. . . .

John Wilcock once said, "Jealousy is one of the easiest emotions to turn off." I used to be jealous. Every woman whom a man found attractive was a threat to me. I had to be all things to a man, to have every desirable attribute a woman could have. It made me very insecure and it was absurd.

Another emotion that assumes the face of jealousy is the hidden fear of failure, the fear that one may not be able to supply the very best, especially in the area of sex. John Williamson highlighted this fear and its resolution in a fictional vignette, in "Sandstone—A Love Community" by Robert Blair Kaiser; it presents a controversial lesson:

Look, I have a wife. We go to bed together. It feels good. I'm scared shitless of losing this because that would deprive me, so I want to own her. I get all involved and neurotic over this ownership. Everything she does I question. I doubt. I don't trust. And so I can't enjoy her any more. She's an object. So I go to a group sex thing. I want to learn that sexual activity by my wife with someone else isn't a threat. I can talk about it, but that doesn't really help the relearning process.

Now, I see her balling someone else, having an obvious good time with a guy who may be ten times better than I perceive myself. All my fears are aroused. Wow! I think he's better than I am, she's going to leave me. It's all over. But it isn't all over. She comes back. Not only hasn't she left me; somehow, mysteriously, our relationship is much better, more turned on. She got rid of her anxiety, she's better for me.

Mimi Lobell ties it all together when she suggests that the key to the problem of jealousy and possessiveness lies in an awareness of the uniqueness of every person:

Everyone is different, and one person's constellation of attractive qualities is a relatively closed system with a harmony and logic of its own. I became aware of style—not as a self-conscious put-on—but as a fact of each person's identity. I learned to reinforce qualities that felt natural to me. This had a two-fold effect. I became more secure in myself as a person, and I was able to see that someone I loved could seek other things in other people who were different from me. Now when John is attracted to another woman, I like to get to know her too. She is apt to be a great person and not to know her would be my loss. . . . People who restrict their loved ones out of insecurity and suspicion never know if the love they receive is given by choice or because they demand it. This is tragic and unnecessary.

The complexities of the emotional adjustment that necessarily surround adapting to an open relationship are such that many other problems are often hidden under the comfortable guise of "jealousy." The tendency to use "jealousy" as a handy catchall was apparent in many responses. One very articulate woman offered a helpful summary of all the personal reactions we received. Thirty years old, top legal secretary, active in community affairs, she unexpectedly found herself and her husband both drawn into intimate satellite relations quite independently during the week of their tenth anniversary.

I thought I would die! (And then miraculously I survived!) My experience is still a new thing to me, and I find time has a way of tempering your inward struggles.

My emotional tensions: Why was I compelled to seek this? Was I promiscuous, childish, etc.? Was it my insecurity in myself as a woman to honestly cope with my innermost feelings toward another man (i.e., performance in bed, etc.)? Couldn't understand jealousy until my husband confided *his* intimate relationship—bringing natural tears, insecurities, possessiveness out into the open. I suddenly realized I wasn't fair in being jealous of his relationship when he tries so hard not to be jealous of mine. Realized that time and energy are problems—these create emotional tensions. I still have conflicts with myself over allotting time to me as an individual to develop, as I have been very unselfish in the past with myself timewise. I'm truly enjoying my development and can accept now a little more than I could at first. Guilt was there (and still is), with *myself,* not at all toward my husband and our marriage, which for all our struggles with this issue, has never been stronger! Yet the risks involved are worth it to me. I feel I am *alive!*

Back to tensions—there is always time to think when one is away and the other knows it and is home alone. I have chosen not to reveal my sexual intimacies to my husband, who has said he would prefer not to know. (I had made my decision before he mentioned this to me.) Originally I wanted to know all about his relationships (womanly curiosity?), but now I find myself asking fewer and fewer questions (and creating less and less tensions). We have opened our communications regarding sexual arousal and I think this will make us more cautious in accepting whatever new situations are presented. I do find myself at times tense with my satellite for fear of getting too involved. A truly unique situation (the growth potential of an open marriage) I'm glad we both found out about before it was too late. Our future: Each day is an experience in living—who knows where we'll end up?

In the reactions cited here, there is a tendency to understate the strong emotions that went into the adjustment.

Most men and women find it difficult to put into words the very personal reactions they experienced. Some men and women simply could not stand the change with all its guilt and tensions. "I couldn't begin to think how I would handle it," one husband admitted. One single woman, involved in a satellite relationship with a married man and his wife, confessed, "I can say that I have never been able to handle the jealousy or insecurity I have in this relationship." Some have turned to an extended family or commune for support, but this is not common.

One conclusion emerges clearly from our rap sessions: very few people can avoid the occasional twinges of jealousy, guilt, and insecurity. They occur at the most inopportune moments, in the oddest situations, because they reflect attitudes that pervade our culture and our traditional pattern of marriage. Sometimes the trigger may be an obvious circumstance, the insecurity of a pregnant wife, a situation that threatens the husband's job, moving to a new community, in fact any radical change that demands all our attention and energies.

■ *Relative Costs*

One question we encountered repeatedly in discussing the problem of jealousy concerned the relative costs of opting for either an Open or Closed Marriage. The Open Marriage has some definite cost factors: it demands constant honest communication, self-searching, analysis of motives, and development of one's identity and independent spirit; it calls for firm resistance to the social conditioning that implies we have only so much love to give and can give it to only one person at a time; it requires that we resist the easy tendency to possess another person and make impossible demands on him or her; it necessitates constant combat with the temptation to be jealous.

In a Closed Marriage, it is easy to be blissfully lulled by the security of believing that against all odds we have found the one and only person who will meet all our needs completely. Peace reigns until the roof caves in and our world is shattered by reality.

The question is whether we prefer to spread our growing pains and adjustments out over several years or to live in a dream world for some years, accepting the odds that it will collapse and we will have to start building a new life. The total cost factor is probably about the same in both open and closed relationships.

Despite this over-all balance in the costs of maintaining Open and Closed Marriages, we believe there are two distinct benefits in the Open Marriage. First, the distribution of the pain of emotional, intellectual, religious, and social adjustment over a period of time creates less stress. Second, the Open Marriage is a growth-oriented relationship.

Weighing the relative costs of Open and Closed Marriages also requires a critical new look at jealousy. Webster defines *jealous* as "watchful or solicitous in guarding or keeping" something or someone. We define jealousy as "an emotional possessiveness rooted in insecurity and fear of loss." Tom Hatfield, of the Sandstone Community, distinguishes between a "time jealousy," expressed in the statement "I don't mind who you're with or what you're doing, but you've been gone too long," and a "selectivity jealousy," expressed in the statement "I don't mind what you're doing or how long you've been gone, but I don't like who you're with." In reality, possessiveness and jealousy can hide under the guise of an Open Marriage. The husband who objects to his wife's spending "too much" time with another man may really be saying to her, "You belong to me and I really don't like sharing you with another." The question of time may be only an excuse for a more subtle message. Trying to select or approve a spouse's friends of the opposite sex can also be a way of expressing possessiveness. It indicates a lack of trust in the partner's judgment of people. The limitations of energy, and of money, can provide other disguised causes for jealousy. If we have to be realistic about the various guises of jealousy and possessiveness, we also have to avoid a naïveté that would suggest unlimited freedom. Carl Rogers rightly warned that "we are limited in the number of deep relationships we can handle because they are so emotionally demanding."

Intimacy and open, honest communications can also become sources of jealousy. The tension between privacy and sharing is very real. How much of one relationship can or ought to be shared in another? Everything? Nothing? Or somewhere between these two extremes? No relationship is ever total, because it involves two unique persons who must retain their unique identity, a core of incommunicable being. The necessity of privacy creates the potential for escaping behind walls. The solution to this tension has to be worked out by each individual and each couple.

Whatever its tenuous biological taproots, jealousy creates a crippling emotion that must be dealt with if we are to grow in our relationships with other persons.

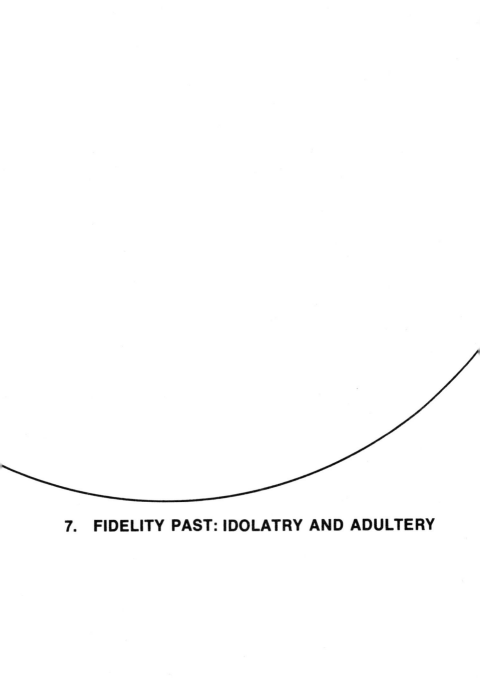

7. FIDELITY PAST: IDOLATRY AND ADULTERY

He who affirms adultery to be the highest breach affirms the bed to be the highest [goal] of marriage, which is in truth a gross and boorish opinion.

—JOHN MILTON

In the new society, paradoxically, sex and sexuality will be both less important and valued more highly. . . . Sex will not be singled out for special emphasis, but since most citizens of the new society will be aware of the vast potential hidden within the domain of sexual experiencing, this facet of self-discovery and self-unfolding will be valued more highly.

—HERBERT OTTO, "Man-Woman Relationships in the Society of the Future"

In this chapter we would like to share with you some of the questions that intrigued us as we tried to sort out the changing views of marital fidelity over the centuries. At first sight, this excursion into theology and history may seem irrelevant, useless. Jessie Bernard, one of America's best-known sociologists of family life, acknowledged recently that "a decreasing number of people see the Bible as anything more than an interesting historical document, as a literature of a romantic nomadic tribe, or at best as a general guide to behavior and ethics that are not specifically relevant and helpful today." Despite this common view, we believe that the theological development of marital fidelity is relevant and helpful, if only it can be seen in the proper perspective of our ongoing evolution as sexual persons.

Six thousand years ago the Semitic world around the Fertile Crescent worshiped a pantheon of gods. One of the most popular of these early tribal gods was El, or Elohim. When Elohim first revealed himself to the patriarchs, he did it in the course of everyday affairs, in simple human form amid their tents and campfires. Sarai was very much at ease talking with El Roi, the God of Vision, about her pregnancy.

In some ways this god of Abram, Isaac, and Jacob was some-what chauvinistic right from the start. He was the God of the Chosen People. But he was also, according to Abram, the "judge of all the earth," "the Lord of all nations." But the god of Moses, Yahweh, revealed himself in the savage wilderness on a craggy mountaintop far above an exiled people. The congenial figure of Elohim gave way to the awe-inspiring holiness and *jealousy* of Yahweh: "I am who am"; "Mount Sinai was all wrapped in smoke, for the Lord came down upon it in fire. The smoke rose from it as though from a furnace, and the whole mountain trembled violently. The trumpet blast grew louder and louder, while Moses was speaking and God answering him with thunder." Yahweh is a jealous god.

The ramifications of this theological evolution from the down-to-earth Elohim to the jealous Yahweh include the concept of marital fidelity. There appears to have been some unconscious, subtle connection among the new concepts of monotheism, Yahweh as a possessive lover, and the shift from the common polygamy of the patriarchs to its gradual extinction.

Elohim was clearly the god of all nations and all peoples. He revealed himself to other nations, even if in some-what veiled form. Elohim, El, or Baal had more than one bride. Israel, to be sure, was his first love, but there were other nations for whom Elohim was God. Abram and the other early patriarchs could easily understand this. When Sarai had no children, Abram took her handmaid Hagar as a consort. Elohim had intimate relations with many nations, just as the patriarchs had many wives and concubines. Many centuries later, Augustine wrote, "Nature allows multiplicity in subjugations, but demands singularity in dominations." In a body you can have many organs subject to one head, but never many heads dominating a single organ. Thus a man could have several wives, but a woman was limited to one husband.

Then Yahweh arrives in fire, thunder, and smoke, the

possessive, jealous God of the Chosen People. One Lord, one bride, dutiful and submissive. Thus patriarchal monogamy replaced patriarchal polygamy. In the earliest matriarchal religions of Egypt, Greece, Phoenicia, and Caanan, creation was seen as some sort of sexual union of the gods. Sex was sacred, and intercourse was a means of achieving union with the divine. Yahweh, the Israelites' god, is celibate. He has no female consort as Tammuz had Ishtar, Osiris had Isis, and Baal had Anath. Creation in Genesis is not a sexual act. The result is a positive demythologizing and desacralizing of human sexuality. The patriarchal aspects of Yahweh would later create many problems, but his celibate creation of the world and man is extremely important. The sexual mysticism of the fertility cults and sacred prostitution had to be abolished as a necessary step toward viewing human sexuality as a freedom that involves persons relating and responding to each other. As Joseph Blenkinsopp suggests, in *Sexuality and the Christian Tradition*:

In the scriptural area of meaning, *man exists as response* both to the call of being and the word which is addressed to him by another. Relational existence means a continual calling into being of the other as I, in my turn, am continually called into being by him. This opens the way to overcoming the dichotomizing of sex as either demonic or institutionalized [in marriage] and to understanding it in the categories of communication, language, address, and response.

Liberated from its mystical aura by the celibate Yahweh, sex was humanized as an essential factor, perhaps the central factor, in our growth as persons.

■ Loving Concern

Within this framework of celibate creation and humanized sex, the personal relationship or covenant—Yahweh's fidelity to his promise, and Abram's faithful response—becomes a vital concept for the evolution of marriage and marital fidelity.

Nearly two thousand years before Christ, the voice of Yahweh came to Abram in the Chaldean land of Ur, promising him a new land. A covenant was made between Abram and Yahweh that Abram and his childless wife would produce countless offspring and rule in a promised land. Years later, when the aged patriarch was commanded to sacrifice his only son, Abram responded with a trust surpassing even what he had shown when he left his father's house to wander in the desert. Fidelity in the Biblical tradition is a terribly complex concept. The fidelity of Yahweh is quite different from Abram's human fidelity. The fidelity of Yahweh is strictly one-sided. No matter what the unfaithful, idolatrous Israelites do, the Lord abides by his commitment. Abram's fidelity, on the other hand, is totally dependent on his trust that Yahweh will be faithful under any circumstance.

Fidelity, 'emet in the Hebrew, very quickly became the main characteristic of God. Though the original derivations of 'emet are not at all certain, most scholars would accept the etymology proposed by Jean Duplacy in the *Dictionary of Biblical Theology*. Duplacy suggests two Hebraic roots for fidelity, or 'emet. One is traced to āman, which suggests solidarity and sureness, and the other to bāṭah, suggesting confidence and security. During and after the Babylonian captivity, some Greek influences probably added to these original root meanings various overtones of hope, confidence, loyalty, belief, truth, and reliability.

Yahweh's fidelity, 'emet, is also often tied in with his paternal concern, ḥesed in Hebrew and *eleos* in Greek. Yahweh made a commitment to care for his people as a father would care for his child. This covenant requires filial devotion and loyalty from the human partner. Human fidelity involves the whole man, and is not just the devoted response of a loyal son to his father. It involves all relationships that a son has— with his family, relatives, friends, and allies. The image we get of fidelity from the Bible, then, is one that focuses on *loving concern, reliability, commitment, solidarity, loyalty, and trust.*

Since the covenant was the central element in everything the Israelites did, it naturally carried over into marriage. Marital fidelity should have been a clear echo of the fidelity outlined here, but that echo was quickly distorted. Marital fidelity was reduced to a sexual exclusivity that applied only to women.

One of the prime factors behind this distortion developed when the patriarchs and prophets of the covenant began to use the relationship of husband and wife to illustrate the covenant between Yahweh and his chosen people.

In the northern kingdom of Galilee during the last years of the tumultuous reign of Jeroboam II (786–746 B.C.), a young priest or cult prophet, Hosea ben Beeri, appeared, a very sensitive, emotional man who could pass quickly from violent anger to the deepest tenderness. Hosea's mission as a prophet in Israel is very much entwined with his own personal tragedy: his painful marriage to Gomer.

Hosea undoubtedly looked upon his young beautiful bride, Gomer, the daughter of Diblaim, as any young husband views his wife, with all the love, romance, and illusion of the newly wed. But the fair wife soon became the faithless wife. Enticed by the pagan rituals of the Canaanites, Gomer became a professional prostitute, perhaps even sharing as a priestess in the sacred prostitution at the temples of Baal. Adultery and idolatry weave together in the story of Gomer and Hosea, for Gomer is a symbol of the infidelity of Israel. In rage over her infidelity, Hosea wanted to divorce his wife, but, just as Yahweh could not renounce Israel, Hosea would take back his wandering wife.

In Hosea's eyes, Israel's infidelity took the form of idolatry and the oppression of the poor, the widowed, and the defenseless. No amount of ritual sacrifice could atone for this infidelity. Yahweh, Israel's bridegroom, would have to strip Israel of her ornaments, the gifts of her false lovers, just as Hosea had treated Gomer. The eleventh chapter of Hosea's prophecy is one of the pinnacles of Old Testament theology. God's loving concern for his chosen people has never been expressed in more moving words. Hosea's experience with Gomer initiated the tradition of describing the relationship between Yahweh and Israel in terms of marriage, a symbolism that later Biblical writers, especially John and Paul, took over in describing the union of Christ and his church.

Gomer's sexual promiscuity subsequently became a handy symbol and analogy for all forms of covenant infidelity, but especially for idolatry. Sometime later, in one of those unmarked transitions in the history of ideas, symbol and reality were inverted. The symbol became the reality. Forgetting these main themes, we became obsessed with sexual infidelity and began condemning extramarital relations, especially on the part of the wife, by equating them with the sinfulness of idolatry.

Parallel with this symbolic inversion are two other developments, one cultural and the other economic. Abram's culture, which traced family lines through the mothers, quickly yielded to a strict patriarchy. The patriarchial structure of the family then produced the images men used to explain the divine and *his* relationship with the Israelites. In Hosea's prophecy and also in the contemporary vocabulary, the word *baal* was used for both the father of the household and the god of the tribe. The Father-King makes the world out of nothing, and the older Mother Goddess of nature is dethroned. Yahweh replaces the Baals, but he cannot get rid of the Mother Goddess as easily as he might want to. She lingers on, transformed into Yahweh's daughter-bride, created and chosen by the Father out of his paternal kindness in return for her exclusive fidelity and obedience. The Mother Goddess becomes the humbled Israel, who naturally yearns for the freedom and position of authority she once held as the consort of Baal. But the husband must win out. Eve did come from Adam's rib. He was made first, she second. And it was Yahweh's decree that women be ruled by their husbands or fathers. As one venerable rabbi put it, "When the husband occupies a chair in paradise, his wife is his footstool."

■ Stolen Property

This cultural patriarchy has economic and legal repercussions that are equally important in understanding the evolution of marital fidelity and the double standard.

In the original version of the Ten Commandments, there is an interesting formula that very much equates the wife with her husband's property: "You shall not covet your neighbor's house, you shall not covet your neighbor's wife, nor his male or female slave, nor his ox or ass, nor anything else that belongs to him." Despite the higher position of women in the Hebraic society relative to that in neighboring societies, the Hebrew woman was still only slightly above the level of chattel and property. In a later version of the Ten Commandments, in the book of Deuteronomy, the wife is listed before her husband's house and other goods, but her position was not greatly changed.

Economically the position of women as subservient property carried over into the legal codes. Adultery for the man meant violating another man's property rights. For the married woman it was a rebellion against her master and a willful violation of his economic and familial interests. If a man seduced or raped a woman already betrothed or married, he could be stoned to death. But this penalty was seldom applied to the man, particularly if he compensated the woman's father or husband for damaging his property. The definition of adultery as whoring clearly placed the prime moral and legal guilt on the woman alone. There were no laws forbidding a man to have intercourse with a liberated woman, one not under some male's protection, unless this involved the risk of idolatry in consorting with sacred prostitutes in the temple of Baal.

The law was much stricter with the woman. If she failed to produce the "tokens of virginity" on her bridal bed, she could be stoned to death. If her husband later suspected her of infidelity, he could drag her before the priests for the gruesome trial of drinking "bitter waters," described in the fifth chapter of the book of Numbers. Another vital factor in the economics of marital fidelity was the concern for the inheritance of flocks and land. The rights of the first-born male were paramount. Maternity could hardly be questioned, but paternity was another matter. Hence the emphasis fell on female virginity and fidelity as safeguards.

In the Christian era, economics continued to be the central factor in marriage and fidelity. Not until the last few hundred years did love become the justification for marriage. When love was firmly believed to be incompatible with marriage, one could hardly expect marital fidelity to be seen in the broad context we described earlier, namely, that of mutual steadfast love. The continued primacy of economics in marriage focused attention on the legal contract concerned with property exchange, community responsibilities, and production of progeny to continue the family line. Marriage consequently became the legal exchange of goods, in church law the mutual exchange of the right to another's body for those acts conducive to procreation. Sexual intercourse became "the marital debt." A spontaneous person-involving act of knowing and response became something a wife put up with to keep her husband from sowing his seed in some other incubator. Paying the marital debt. Ultimately, the strength and validity of the marriage contract itself became totally dependent on delivery of the goods. A marriage ceremony in church was not sufficient to create an indissoluble union. Bodies, female in particular, had to be delivered on the marital bed at least once to consummate the contract.

When the whole foundation of the male-female relationship rested on economics, the husband's extramarital affairs posed no real threat to his marriage. Economics was the only complication considered, and this could usually be handled to the mutual satisfaction of the two males, the aggrieved and the trespasser.

■ Northern Affairs

In the past four hundred years, since the Protestant Reformation, two main social models have crystallized, rooted in geographic differences. In Spain, Italy, and much of France, the traditional economic basis of marriage blended with the courtly love code to produce a model that is still quite common. Morton Hunt, in The Affair, labels this pattern the pagan-courtly model. Marriage remains primarily an institution designed for social benefit, and does not involve an emotional romantic involvement. The exuberance of sex bursts forth in the extramarital relationship. For the middle and upper classes, the mistress has become a socially accepted reality. The lover and mistress have certain dignity that Americans and northern Europeans find hard to understand. Among the lower classes the romantic courtly love attitudes seem to have little influence. Economics, family arrangements, and casual uninvolved physical sex are the dominant concerns there. In northern Europe, however, the pagan-courtly model has strongly influenced the behavior of the aristocracy and royalty. The concept of romance between a man and a woman was perfectly acceptable, but the northern temperament was uneasy with the courtly love code and the southern acceptance of adultery as a reward for love. The solution was to shift the object of romance from the wife of someone else to the single woman, and then to one's own wife. Thus emerged the puritan-bourgeois tradition of marriage. Love and marriage were wedded to create the most meaningful and intimate of all human relationships. Romance, sex, and parenthood became the hallmarks of true marriage. As the Protestants came to accept divorce, the extramarital relationship became a mortal enemy of marriage and society because it was often the prelude to and cause for divorce. Society responded by defending marriage and the family as the rock foundations of everything we hold dear. The message was clear: one cannot possibly truly love one's spouse and be sexually unfaithful. Result for the affair: guilt, conflict, secrecy, and the choice between an occasional purely physical encounter and a deeply emotional relationship that must inevitably supplant the marriage. In a recent *McCall's* magazine survey, 70 per cent of the respondents were convinced that any sexual infidelity is self-evident proof that one does not really love his or her spouse.

Basically, Americans have opted for the northern European puritan-bourgeois model. We have canonized it as the only acceptable model for adults. In a few enclaves—among the aristocratic rich, the bohemian artists, the jet set—the pagan-courtly model is followed. In the upper classes of American society, the discreet love affair may be tacitly considered a component of marriage, as with Franklin D. Roosevelt, Joseph P. Kennedy, Sr., and Warren G. Harding.

Today the socially approved puritan-bourgeois model seems to serve the emotional needs and abilities of only a small minority of Americans, if we are to judge from divorce and infidelity statistics. In our fragmented, impersonal culture, the romantic exclusive marriage provides an island of emotional stability and security for both husband and wife, yet it is ill-adapted to our increasing life expectancies, mobility, and equalization of the sexes. In reality the deviant and socially rejected pagan-courtly model seems much better suited to the majority of Americans.

The advantages of the disapproved model have been neatly highlighted by Morton Hunt, but with a subtle Hot Sex bias toward the male. The pagan-courtly model, with its acceptance of the affair, offers a functional pattern for renewal within the marriage, personal excitement, and the challenge of continued growth. But infidelity is both expensive and time consuming. It conflicts with the home-based habits of our middle-class society. It can be socially and professionally hazardous. It can also be psychologically risky and traumatic. Morton Hunt sums it up by suggesting that, while high life expectancy and other factors are making fidelity increasingly difficult and restrictive of personal growth, the secretive affair is becoming less and less practical.

■ So Where Are We?

In the past hundred years, the sentimental Victorian models of marriage and family have been undermined by the sexual revolution and the demise of family self-sufficiency. The ideal of female fidelity has been transformed into one of mutual marital fidelity. But reality has created an impasse. As women became the equals of men, they began to expect the same fidelity of their husbands that had previously been demanded only of them. Drawn by the beauty of the Victorian model of woman, man accepted this expectation in principle if not in practice. Marriage became a genuinely mutual pact, with sexual exclusivity the standard for both husband and wife. When reality does not match the ideal, the only honest and practical solution is divorce and remarriage, or a new definition of mutual fidelity and commitment. If we do not redefine fidelity, then our standard of sexual exclusivity will continue to encourage serial monogamy as the prevalent pattern of male-female relationship.

It seems clear that we cannot solve the tensions between our radically changed ecosystem and our ideal of lifelong sexual fidelity within the puritan-bourgeois model of sentimental togetherness. Serial monogamy, with its easy acceptance of divorce and several mates during a lifetime, hardly seems adapted to developing truly intimate knowing relationships between men and women. Divorce and remarriage may serve to mature some, but for most it simply means returning to the frustrating merry-go-round of impossible Hot Sex expectations. Swingers may gain some time and advantage with their modified concept of fidelity and their safety valve of physical variety, but the basic values remain the same as those of the serial monogamist.

The question then is: Do we want to continue along the

path we have trod for several centuries, a path that clearly appears to be getting more and more impassable? Or are we willing to venture some new definitions? Is there perhaps a better, more functional, more growth-oriented way of looking at fidelity between men and women other than as simple sexual exclusivity?

8. FIDELITY TODAY: TWO IN ONE FLESH OR TWO IN ONE SPIRIT?

Sexual adventures outside marriage are certainly a betrayal of the most intimate commitment that two human beings can make to each other and it is absurd to pretend otherwise. . . . We dare not detach sexual relations from the particular context of the monogamous marriage, actual or prospective.
—PAGE SMITH, *Daughters of the Promised Land*

Fidelity without a sense of diversity can become an obsession and a bore; diversity without a sense of fidelity, an empty relativism.
—ERIK ERIKSON

Faithfulness is not simply a matter of faithfulness to others, but first of all a matter of faithfulness to oneself—a power to define oneself from within and to remain constant to that self-definition. In the last analysis, faithfulness is the power of personhood.
—HERBERT RICHARDSON, *Nun, Witch, Playmate*

The mating animal is driven by the primal instincts of sexual heat and sexual aggression to a union whose sole function and purpose is continuation of the species. There is no personal communion, no love among animals. This primal sexual aggression extends into the human domain, symbolized in the Biblical metaphor "They became two in one flesh." As long as early man saw himself primarily in terms of a body, sexual aggression and domination of the male over the female could continue as the highest mode of human union possible. But humans also have a capacity to love, and with a growing awareness of ourselves as sexual persons, a new and higher alternative became available. Men and women could finally transcend their primeval sexual aggressions and submissions to become two in one spirit.

■ Psychological Fidelity

The possibility of transcending the body yet remaining within it has produced the present conflicts over the meaning of fidelity. Transcendence leads us to a new perspective in which fidelity is essentially integrated with our developing capacity for intimacy with other persons.

All of us experience many forms of love, starting with our attachment to our mothers, our childhood friendships, and expanding family attachments. Puberty brings a fresh force into these relationships triggered by the heightened levels of hormone synthesis. The earliest experiences males have of their sexual drive are those of primal sexual aggression: the teasing and the conquering, or taking. The intimacy of human sexuality comes from a mutual sharing that gives initiative and responsiveness to both persons. Thus sexual aggression and domination exist only when the individuals involved do not experience themselves and their partners as persons. The ancient world accepted this primal pattern of union. It drew on our ancestral reservoir of anxiety and aggression in a way that made true friendship between men and women impossible. Courtly love began the revolution against this primal pattern. Friendship could now exist because the ancient patriarchal hierarchy of male over female was inverted.

In early adolescence, the young male's capacity of relating to another sexual person is embryonic. Moved by hormones, he relates in the primal way with aggression and dominance. As maturity and identity as a sexual person develop, he gradually transforms this primal sexual desire into love. He is no longer driven by the biological need to assure the survival of his species or his family line. Nor is his prime motive any longer a private enjoyment or even mutual orgasm. A desire to know another more fully as a person must eventually come to take precedence over the simple desire for sexual union.

The adolescent relation of young men and women is very much limited by their undeveloped personalities. The key to more mature relations lies in going beyond our primal drives and developing a facility and skill in communional love and friendship. But, as Teilhard de Chardin remarked in

The Divine Milieu, "in order to be united, you must first of all be yourself as completely as possible." Faithfulness to oneself is a prime requisite to our growth as autonomous persons and our relations with other persons. First we must separate ourselves from our family, learning to define and assert our self-dependence as free adults. This painful and gradual growth, spread over many years and, for some, over a lifetime, requires the development of three virtues, according to Herbert Richardson: fidelity, competence, and sharing love.

Richardson's treatment of the virtues of competence, fidelity, and sharing love deviates from the schema originally proposed by Erik Erikson in *Insight and Responsibility*. Erikson placed competence among the childhood virtues and love among the adult virtues. However, Richardson modifies these schema to bring the three virtues into the psychosexual development of the adolescent. He does not note his deviation from Erikson and clearly implies that his own schema is that of Erikson. In our framework, the Richardson schema is more functional, hence our use of it.

Fidelity in psychological terms is the power to define oneself from within and not in terms of roles imposed from without. Fidelity requires the growing ability to remain constant to our own self-definition. Psychological fidelity is primarily a faithfulness to oneself. But it is equally a faithfulness to others, an expanding willingness to accept the self-definitions other persons make in their evolution toward autonomous personhood.

In a patriarchal authoritarian culture, fidelity in the sense we have defined it is a vice. The adolescent and even the adult are not encouraged to develop their own self-definitions. Laurence Wylie illustrates this pattern in his comparison of "Youth in France and the United States":

The average French child (and his parents even more than he) has a clear idea of the limits within which his ambitions may be fulfilled. He knows to what social and professional class he belongs. There is no doubt about his family's traditional, political, religious, and even aesthetic ideals, and he has been placed by both family and teachers in a well-defined intellectual category.

His identity comes from the roles set forth by the elders and society.

This is the problem *The Graduate* faced when he returned from college. His parents, following a patriarchal code, tried to give him an identity: a sporty car, a job in his father's firm. The popularity of this movie can be traced to its basic message: to be an adult in today's world, Benjamin must seek self-definition under his own power.

In a patriarchal culture such as the French, the adolescent's identity as a sexual person is also imposed by his elders. His ability to perform as a male must be certified by an older, sexually experienced woman. Once so certified, the new patriarch can in turn initiate a younger woman, ideally his virgin wife. Mrs. Robinson seduces Bejamin to certify his performance ability, and then tries to direct his relations with his girl friend. But Benjamin realizes that he cannot accept his sexual identity from anyone. He has to create it himself with his equally inexperienced girl friend. He must be faithful to himself and his girl by risking the dangers of self-discovery through self-experience.

In degenitalizing sexual relations, courtly love laid the foundation for today's youth's challenge to define their identity. It recognized the value of sexual foreplay in its own right, rather than as a prelude to genital intercourse. We can fault the troubadours' scorn for sexual intercourse, but their emphasis on the value of the pure kiss, the chaste touch, celibate fondling, and even naked contact of true lovers has made possible the present American pattern of extended courtship in a prolonged adolescence. It has also set the stage for developing three new adolescent virtues: competence, fidelity, and sharing love.

The prolonged adolescence of American youth, with its

extended courtship and dating pattern, provides a world in which they can gradually explore and develop competence and skill in physical communication. With a diffused degenitalized sexuality, today's youth are free to explore at their own pace the intimacies of holding hands and fond glances, petting and fondling, and the more committed modes of genital communication. Thus they can easily match their level of psychosexual intimacy with their development as persons. Erikson suggests that the adolescent can hardly be expected to handle the fullest sexual mutuality and intimacy. The Roys have also warned about the harmful effects of sexual intercourse on adolescents who engage in it before their personal identities are well established. The American pattern of extended dating plays an important role in developing the adolescent virtues of fidelity and sharing love "by encouraging persons," as Richardson suggests, "to engage in limited, though progressively more intimate and involving, commitments. In the course of this learning, we lay the foundation for a new and broader expression of fidelity in marriage, in all the relations we have with other persons, and in faithfulness to our own self-definition."

■ *New Definitions*

In our informal survey we were repeatedly told that marital fidelity means an exclusive love-sexual relationship between one man and one woman. Or, more tersely, fidelity is "sexual exclusivity." Many couples, however, try to be more realistic. They can accept an occasional indiscretion, provided it is infrequent and only physical. Women tend to make this adaptation more often than men, perhaps in a quiet nod to the double moral standard.

The picture is harder to define if one looks at marital fidelity in terms other than sexual exclusivity. Our inquiry regarding the new definition of *marital fidelity* in America today brought a variety of interesting responses. Since the responses came out of personal experiences, we would like

to present some of the more representative answers in their
original form.

At Sandstone Retreat, John Williamson echoed the uneasiness of many with the hidden expectation implied by the
word *fidelity:*

I would no longer use the term *fidelity* because, stretched
to its limits, it implies and defines a static structure of expectations and behavior which cannot help but come into
conflict with living processes. This static structure can
only prevent or hinder a person's potential in an ongoing
life of experience. I prefer to replace *fidelity* with something like *commitment* or *bond,* which allows for a continual
movement beyond the present. We need a word that
projects or symbolizes the binding factor of a dynamic,
developing relationship. Commitment to me is literally an
act of faith. Knowing where I stand in terms of my own
unique needs, weaknesses, strengths, and potentials, I
offer this self to another person, to the forces of change
and to an unknown future. The act of faith, of course,
comes only after I have interacted with another person
and found that a mutuality exists which will or can be
reinforcing. Such an act of faith truly opens the door to
trust, acceptance, and understanding. It allows for fusion
without threat, merging without dependence, and the
creation of a new order of being. Without this faith or
commitment, for me at least, there is no growth or joy or
goodness or new energy, only a mechanical acting out of
needs which are never fulfilled.

Barbara Williamson was even more strongly opposed to
using the word *fidelity.* She defined the phrase *marital fidelity* as an anachronism that "should be eliminated," and offered the following alternatives:

1. Sexually nonexclusive.
2. Respect for the needs of each person—not having two
   people smother each other.

3. Allowing each person to be an individual and not an object.

4. Eliminating a parasitic dependence and allowing interdependence.

Commitment, for her, is everything. "Commitment establishes a base of security, trust, and desire to work through problems together."

After ten years of marriage, one woman in her early thirties expressed her views on fidelity against the background of a brief comarital relationship:

A faithfulness to my husband and myself [means] to allow each other the freedom to grow as individuals. A faithfulness to observe the loyalties we feel toward family, friends, business associates, etc., and keep them in proper perspective. Marital fidelity is based on the open communications between husband and wife that allow you to really see yourself honestly, with a trust and understanding of the forces which may drive us to react differently than we had ever thought possible. The security of a home and a husband who knows me possibly better than I know myself is important to me. I feel a strong responsibility to give myself completely to my role as wife, mother, confidant, lover, friend, etc. I am committed totally to keeping the marriage I have.

When we asked her to explain commitment, she defined it in the total framework of her life rather than within the marital context:

A commitment to living involves a commitment to people. I assume you're referring to relationships with the opposite sex and so my answer is in this context. My commitment in my interpersonal relationships is so total at times it is mind-boggling! I am amazed at myself that I can become so concerned that I would seemingly walk to the ends of the earth for that person, yet not feel a guilt toward my husband and our primary relationship. I need interpersonal relationships on many varying levels and hope I am fortunate enough to be able to enjoy them as time passes. I can quickly determine now whether a new relationship could have possible meaning, and be honest with myself instead of channeling out my feelings.

Some of our respondents were uneasy with the term "commitment":

Sometimes the word comes on too strong to me, mainly because I get the feeling that this word means a bond which can never be broken in any way after it is made. By saying "I have committed myself to this person," I seem to be saying also, "therefore I must do everything and anything for him that he wishes." By avoiding this strong bond feeling, I feel that commitment means an entrustment to another's care. To be able to belong to a relationship in which each partner is "committed" to know and understand the other.

This same young woman saw marital fidelity as "unconditional loyalty and loving concern, a mutuality."

■ *Composite Picture*

The following is a composite picture of fidelity distilled from our respondents' reactions:

Caring for and loving one another, physically and emotionally.
Treating each other as individuals.
Trusting, being truthful.
Thinking of each other's wants and needs.
Being true to the contract we agreed upon, oral or written.
Not necessarily precluding extramarital relationships as long as primary relationship is maintained and strengthened.
Being honest. People relate to one another on many dif-

ferent levels, and deceit on any one of these levels, not just the sexual, is infidelity. Being completely open. Listening to one another.

Being open to a kind of craziness, recognizing that if we are thoroughly rational at all times we will lose faith in ourselves, our partners, or chances of relying on anybody for life.

Keeping perspective, refusing to take or be taken all that seriously.

Doing the unexpected, at least now and then. We constantly surprise those to whom we are faithful simply because we are listening or revealing things we ourselves didn't know about ourselves. An unfaithful partner is one who doesn't believe in surprises, has no time for the wild thing on a moment's notice, looks always for reasons.

Respecting the dignity of the partner, being willing to accept gratefully all that the other is and is becoming, accepting the wonder of what is.

The picture we have developed of commitment parallels very closely the respondents' definitions of fidelity. In the more traditional vein, many stated that commitment, like fidelity in marriage, means one thing: sexual exclusivity. Some also suggested that it "means total and complete dedication to the welfare of the other person, and absolute devotion to the principle of marital fidelity defined as sexual exclusivity," or "a sense of dedication, including marital fidelity, supporting his physical and psychological well-being, dedicating a certain portion of my ego to him."

One couple in their early thirties have been wrestling with the question of fidelity and commitment within what appears to be a very open yet sexually exclusive relationship. The husband admitted he would find it hard to cope with his emotions should his wife develop a satellite sexual relationship. We thought this a bit pessimistic, and perhaps an overly cautious appraisal of his own abilities to handle change in a very healthy, open primary relationship. His wife, however, shared with us some rich insights into her concepts of fidelity and commitment that very much bridged the traditional and the new:

Fidelity means that the two persons within the marriage bond have reserved a "special" part of themselves for their partner. They know the best and the worst of each other—yet they genuinely "like" each other. They are each other's best friend. The partners achieve the expression of this single and unique love through "sexual exclusivity."

In my marriage, my "commitment" is to accept my responsibility of fulfilling my so-called roles of wife, mother, and [school] teacher in my daily life. Since my roles vary, I realize that my husband's also vary. We share some of these roles, such as child raising, contributing to our family finances, and menial chores in the home. We also have a "commitment" to each other, such as giving each other comfort, understanding, and sharing good and bad times. But because we are involved with other people of the opposite sex in our daily lives, we have both developed friendships with these individuals. We both have common friends and our own circles of friends. I have experienced no difficulty with these interpersonal relationships, or in developing future friendships.

Her husband was a little more apprehensive about his friendships and business contacts with women, and conceded that he was always "somewhat guarded" in these relationships, "since I don't want to give a woman the feeling that I am trying to pick her up, or mentally making her."

In general we found that the newer images of commitment included some common elements, despite the variation in experiences and perspectives:

Loving, sharing, helping each other, concerned interest.
Caring enough about someone not to hurt him in any way if at all possible. Honesty and total concentration on the person you are with at the time.

Being very personal, striving to keep our love strong and
real. In essence, my commitment to others is to let them
know where I stand.

Making sure nothing is hidden. Responsibility for my actions
and relations with any individual.

Being unselfish—when love becomes strong enough so that
the other person's wishes really do come first, I believe
the commitment is total. Of course, this can be over-
done.

Giving the relationship "first call." Wanting to make the relationship work, not just hoping it will work.

Having mutual understanding, support, love, discretion. We
protect each other's vulnerability. Total acceptance, no
matter what pains we've caused each other. Not fan-
tasizing about what might be.

Fulfilling my definition of *marital fidelity* (caring for and loving one another, treating each other as persons, trust
and honesty, and thinking of each other's wants and
needs) and being honest with everyone.

Toward the end of *Open Marriage,* Nena O'Neill and
George O'Neill focus on the essence of the old and new definitions of *fidelity.*

Sexual fidelity is the false god of closed marriage, a god
to whom partners submit (or whom they defy) for all the
wrong reasons and often at the cost of the very relationship which that god is supposed to protect. Sex in the
closed marriage is envisioned in terms of fidelity, thus
becoming the be-all and end-all of love, instead of being
seen in its proper perspective as only one facet of the
much larger reality of love. Fidelity in the closed marriage is the measure of *limited* love, *diminished* growth and
conditional trust. This fixation in the end defeats its own
purpose, encouraging deception, sowing the seeds of mis-
trust and limiting the growth of both partners and so of
the love between them.

Fidelity, in its root meaning, denotes allegiance and
fealty to a duty or obligation. But love and sex should

never be seen in terms of duty or obligation, as they are in closed marriage. They should be seen as experiences to be shared and enjoyed together.

Fidelity today has become a matter of choice between the possessive and insecure exclusivity of two in one flesh and the open and inclusive trust of two in one spirit.

PART THREE

TRANSITIONS

9. FEMALE REBELLIONS AND SOCIAL INVERSIONS

Our tragic adventure in Vietnam may be traced to outmoded ideals of "manliness" as well as to considerations of international strategy.
—GEORGE B. LEONARD, "Why We Need a New Sexuality"

Even the catch-all notion of a sexual revolution offers false comfort, for it presupposes a revolution limited to sexuality whereas in reality it embraces all of life, society, art, and lunges forward into a future that is completely discontinuous with the past.
—IRVING BUCHEN, *The Perverse Imagination: Sexuality and Literary Culture*

If one were to turn our puny earth into a star with the same brilliant mass of the sun, one would turn our solar system into shambles. In time, gravity would reshuffle the planets, moons, and comets to produce a new orderly system. We believe that today's liberation of women and the current sexual revolution are capable of creating similar drastic changes in our society, producing total havoc and restructuring our social system economically, politically, and legally. Change the position of women in society, and you change the whole system, the whole organization of our lives.

■ *Corporate State Marriage*

For centuries men have dominated life in the Western world. The world has been defined in their masculine terms and images. Women today have to be defined in their own right, distinct and independent of the male role and identity. On all social levels, except that of the black lower class, wives have depended on their husbands for their status and position in society. Men have always struggled for equal status with other men rather than with women. Somehow they have assumed that if they have equality as individual males, their women will share in this equality and all its benefits. A male's economic independence and security are shared by his wife, but the reality of this shared equality is much like the light and heat of the sun reflected by the moon. As long as women are economically dependent on men and socially indistinguishable from them, they will always be relative creatures, designed to be supportive of the male.

In its Hot Sex fear of human sexuality, the patriarchal culture has placed a prime emphasis on rendering sex and the female safe behind the institutional walls of monogamy. The French writer Montherlant expressed women's relative existence within marriage when he wrote, "The man who gets married always makes a gift to the woman, because she has need of marriage and he does not. . . . Woman is made for man, and man is made for life."

Independence for life is the traditional lot of the male, while marital-maternal dependence is the fate of the female. Even in recent decades, when young men and women have begun to enjoy the advantages of single adult life, marriage remains the ultimate goal for the majority of women, regardless of background and education. For men, marriage merely adds another dimension to their lives, an intimate relationship and home base, some new responsibilities. For women, marriage means that the outside world and the interests for which she has been trained and educated are now subordinated to her marital and maternal responsibilities. When a man marries, he does not give up his job or move to his spouse's home. His roots remain intact. It is the wife whose life is changed. If she lives some distance from him, she is automatically expected by everyone, including herself, to pack up her things, wave good-by to her friends, quit her job, however rewarding it might be financially or psychologically. She may or may not be able to continue her career when she is re-established in her new home, but that is secondary to her new identity. Her husband's employment is the basis of his independence and her very relative "independence." The new home may be challenging and rewarding for the wife, but it is not her free choice. It is, as Elizabeth Janeway so bluntly put it, "man's world, woman's place."

Or, in the biting commentary of Alexis de Tocqueville in his study of democracy in America:

The independence of women is irrevocably lost in the bonds of matrimony. If an unmarried woman is less constrained [in America] than elsewhere, a wife is subjected to stricter obligations. The former makes her father's house an abode of freedom and pleasure; the latter lives in the home of her husband as if it were a cloister.

The changing function of the family in today's postindustrial societies is also creating problems for women in terms of the male world. The industrial system has alienated productive work from the home, leaving the domesticated female with an endless cycle of housekeeping drudgeries and the limited creativities of maternal joys and duties. In the past, women had the contact and challenge of a dozen children, however infant-oriented that world may have been. Today, this task of socializing and educating children is shared with outside agencies. The married woman's world continually shrinks. Her role seems to be primarily satisfying those needs of her family that cannot be met by any outside agency.

In *The Greening of America,* Charles Reich summed up the new roles of the family, and indirectly pinpointed the problem of new definitions and functions for the married woman:

It is ironic that the form of community most praised and cherished by American society, the family, has probably suffered the greatest destruction at the hands of the Corporate State. Technology has deprived the family of almost all of its functions. The family has no work to do together, no mutual education. The State wants the family to be a unit for consumption, to exist for the purpose of watching television, using leisure products and services, and living the life of false culture. The State wants its consuming units as small as possible; were it not for certain biological necessities for which substitutes have not yet come into use, the solitary individual would be the best possible unit for the [postindustrial] State's purposes.

The advent of children can add a new dimension to the relative definition of woman. Its joyous dimensions are mixed with bewildering tensions and problems for the new mother. The new father shares the joys but few of the bewildering tensions. Fatherhood is another enriching facet added on to the male's life. Motherhood becomes the all-consuming central reality of the woman's life. Psychologically and financially, parenthood adds to a man's responsibilities. For a woman it means increased psychological and financial dependence on her husband. A man's leisure time traditionally belongs to himself; a woman's leisure traditionally belongs to her family. Thus, in many ways, parenthood expands a man's world and constricts his wife's.

In past generations women gladly accepted this state of affairs because they could not exist alone in a world where men controlled finances and productive work. Now, with women being educated as individuals, they are increasingly turning to their own personal needs, their own interests, their own identities, just as men have done in the past.

Our technology and our educational system have contributed to this trend. Our children are indoctrinated with a consumer-leisure mentality long before they become financially independent. As a result, long before our children leave home, they have been consumers in their own right. This accelerates the return of the family to its original couple state, but with the vital difference that the husband has continued to grow, while the wife is left with little beyond her empty nursery.

■ *Community*

Two is better than one, but in today's world it is not enough. We need a sense of community and belonging. The family has shrunk from a tribe of fifteen or twenty individuals to a frightened quartet searching and struggling for intimacy in an impersonal world. The sterile conversations at typical middle-class dinners and cocktail parties, the frenzied pursuit of youth and sexy romance, the togetherness leisure activities of skiing, boating, and collecting, the many organizations and groups that create the illusion of togetherness out of proximity cannot compensate for the sense of belonging lost in the struggle to accumulate and consume more and more material goods.

Men and women both need the stimulation and variety of contacts outside the home. But for the woman this pressing need is not answered by the traditional roles of wife and mother. Meeting this need has to wait until these socially imposed supportive roles, especially that of motherhood, have been met. Only then can a wife seek the fulfillment and experience, the freedom of self-definition, her husband has never ceased to enjoy.

The possibilities for women to expand their outside contacts come at different times in different marriages. For some they come when the youngest child goes off to school; for others, when the couple decide to have no more children, when the youngest child enters adolescence, when the youngest is finally married, or when the thirtieth or fortieth birthday rolls around.

When a woman finally makes the decision to go beyond her primary relational identity as wife and mother, she is bound to create tensions within her marriage. New modes of activity, new ways of relating are tried out. These will force the husband and wife to adjust their own relationship. They must be more outspoken and honest when they try expressing what they really value in their relationship and what they seek to find in it. Candor and honesty may be hard for the traditionally submissive wife, who may feel guilty over her "rebellious ingratitude." The tacit assumptions and expectations with which the couple began their relationship are no longer valid. New expectations must be articulated, and ways of meeting them discovered.

Though we like to deny it, women who go beyond their

relational roles create anxieties, however subconscious or subliminal. New interpersonal relationships are bound to affect the primary relationship of husband and wife. The self-definition of women thus extends its effects to society at large.

When a woman steps outside the home, she creates at least one major practical problem in her marriage. In his study *Sexual Bargaining: Power Politics in the American Marriage,* John Scanzoni shows that the vast majority of working wives are still caught in their relational definitions. A working wife continues to provide the domestic base and support her husband expects; she does the laundry, the housecleaning, the shopping, the cooking. She may work full time, but she is still expected to have dinner on the table at the usual hour. This has to change if the working wife is not to be doubly exploited.

When a woman steps outside her relational definitions of mother and wife, she needs the same psychological support from her husband she has traditionally given him. But she needs it more than he does, because she is violating her traditional social roles in working, while he is only fulfilling his. If a husband truly values his wife as an individual, he will actively encourage her to satisfy these needs. He will make the necessary adjustments in his own life style, goals, and work expectations to accommodate the changing life style of his wife. This will require a greater sharing of the domestic chores, more mutual involvement in the rearing of the children. An understanding, honest husband will appreciate his wife's need for the free time she must have to find and establish herself. Most of all, her need will require adjustment in his way of thinking, so that he will not interpret the expansion of his wife's life as a threat to his identity and ego.

Most women do not want to forsake motherhood and married life, but they do want to balance these supportive roles with more creative and fulfilling challenges outside the home. To accomplish this effectively, they have to persuade their husbands to share familial and occupational roles. In fact, the future will have to allow for more role inter-changeability. When many women become as career-oriented as their husbands, and their job status and incomes roughly equal, wives will be able to achieve equal status and power in marriage.

Many men view the possible equalization of the sexes as a direct threat to their manhood. A woman's decision to take a job often produces violent and suppressed tensions that not infrequently break through to the surface in direct confrontations and ultimatums. In the future, women, we hope, will have the first say in determining their careers, but today that determination, unfortunately, still lies largely with the husband. Scanzoni argues that the "long-term changes in marital forms in general, as well as changes in the frequency of divorce, are largely the result of female pressures for greater equity of rewards against male resistance to give up their ancient prerogatives." Unhappily, if a woman wants to avoid serious conflicts and possibly even divorce today, she has to maneuver her husband's consent, approval, and support. No one has ever given up power willingly and without the pressure of persuasion and necessity. This holds true in families just as it does in politics and business.

The ideal situation, of course, is one in which the husband does not need much persuasion. An understanding male can take the edge of guilt off the adjustment for both. He can also reduce the mental and physical fatigue his wife will experience.

■ *Children*

Once the two individuals in a marriage have accepted each other and a particular life style, their children will accept the consequences of that life style. They will accept a mother's staying at home and finding fulfillment there. They will equally accept a mother who works or has a career of her own. They will accept all the minor adjustments that have to be made, all the familial difficulties involved in this life style, if the couple themselves have accepted these adjustments and difficulties willingly and happily. However, the children will not accept a way of life they sense their parents are not comfortable with. It works both ways. Children will sense the underlying frustration of their mother's unsatisfied needs. A wife who is denied self-definition by her husband can turn to her children, projecting her goals and needs on them. The end result is anxiety and disappointment for all.

The immediate problem faced by a working mother is providing alternative supervision and care for her children. A father never worries about this because it is automatically assumed that the wife cares for the children. But a working mother removes that support system, and in that case both father and mother must face the task of child care, either themselves or with the aid of others. Few working women can stagger their employment so that at least one parent is always home to care for the children. If the children are of school age, someone must still be home to get them off to school in the morning and care for them when they come home in the afternoon. Sometimes supervised activities at school will occupy the children until their parents return from work. Grandparents, relatives, or neighbors are sometimes willing to serve as a sort of semiprofessional parent for an hour or two five days a week. If the couple's joint salaries can handle the added expense of one of these arrangements, this may provide the essential solution. Day-care centers or nursery schools are other possibilities. But these are far too few to meet today's needs. And they are not likely to become more common in the next few years. The collapse of federal support for expanding day-care centers in 1972 and 1973, because these "would not promote the traditional values of the American family," does not bode much hope for the social support structures our changing families and marriages require to function and adjust efficiently.

During World War II, industries set up nurseries to take advantage of the female labor pool. After the war, they were discontinued as the working mother made room for the returning soldier. Some companies in suburban areas have set up small preschool centers to tap the labor force available among educated and skilled housewives. In the southern states, similar day-care centers have been provided by industry. Whether this will become a trend is a moot point, though industry will have to respond as the number of single workers with children increases. One child in six in the United States is already in the custody of a single parent, divorced, widowed, or unmarried.

■ Male Friends

Once a husband has accepted his wife's need to define herself, and once the problem of child rearing has been resolved satisfactorily, one final problem remains for the couple. While the wife remains at home, her husband serves as a filter, separating her from the outside world. Specifically, he has near-complete control over the men she meets socially. But once she ventures outside her domestic circle, her contacts and experiences are uniquely her own. She will meet new people, form friendships with people her husband does not even know. Many of these new friends will be men. How will her husband react to the knowledge that his wife is in contact with men he doesn't know? Will he take his wife's new friendships as a threat and fill his head with fantasies of his naïve wife being led astray? Will he fear that his wife will compare him with her friends? Or will he accept her new friendships with trust? Will he be able to accept his wife's acquaintances for what they are?

In developing the open friendships that are part of the self-definition many women are exploring today, husbands and wives must be candid and honest in discussing the different forms her new acquaintances will take. Most of these acquaintances will remain casual; some will grow into close friendships that both husband and wife will share; others will grow into close friendships the husband may not share. Some may become intimate enough to be called emotional and loving relationships; some may even involve sexual expression. All of these possibilities have to be faced with trust in each other and in the strength of the primary bond.

■ *Social Reforms*

Thus far we have concentrated on the emergence of women in relation to their husbands and children. However, the repercussions go much further than the individual family circle. They are echoed in the sexual practices of the whole society and its religiopolitical outlook.

The advent of the romantic marriage forced a total restructuring of society a hundred years ago. It destroyed the age-old patriarchal subordination of female to male and set up an essential equality as the basis for male-female relationships. It displaced the parent-child relationship from a primary to a secondary position, with the husband-wife relationship now dominant. It encouraged the development of individuality for women. It became, in the words of Herbert Richardson, the "cradle of democratic feeling, the seedbed of opposition to traditional [patriarchal] authority." The patriarchal family can only survive and thrive, according to a contemporary European political thinker, Dietrich Haensch, in totalitarian political systems. It obviously cannot survive in our culture, even in a romanticized Victorian form.

Our advanced postindustrial culture has created an environment in which brains are clearly the chief criterion for economic independence. This puts women on a par with men, and makes it possible for them to achieve the economic independence essential to their self-definition as unique individuals.

Richardson's brilliant and careful study of the Americanization of sex summarizes the social revolution hidden in the supposedly limited sexual revolution:

The American romantic marriage and the parent/child [two-generation] family cannot be regarded as the fulfill-

ment of this evolutionary process, if only because these
institutions are tightly bound up with an aggressive-pos-
sessive economic system that must also be superseded if
man is to survive. It is important to realize that the attitudes, virtues, and goals presupposed by aggressive-pos-
sessive capitalism do tend to form a person who possesses
only a limited capacity for personal intimacy and hetero-
sexual sharing. (The Women Liberationists are correct in
their estimate that American capitalism is patriarchal, for
hierarchical patriarchy reinforces the competitive orienta-
tion that thinks in terms of moving "higher" and getting
"ahead.") What this means, therefore, is that there is a
disequilibrium among American institutional ideals. A
highly competitive [consumerist] economy reinforces re-
sidual patriarchal, nonequalitarian tendencies in the sexual sphere—where such patriarchal tendencies run contrary to the professed personal-romantic idea. This
disequilibrium will gradually be corrected by the
emergence of new communal forms of economic organization.

The "emergence of new communal forms of economic
organization" that Herbert W. Richardson, Rosemary
Ruether, Rosemary Haughton, Shulamith Firestone, Gordon
Rattray Taylor, and many others forecast will require a radical
change in the current middle-class urban-suburban ecosystem. That system reflects the interdependence of the working male and the domesticated female. A woman who wants
to be married and have a career must, in this system, juggle
two jobs simultaneously.

It is only in a totally new system, a completely restructured society, that the evolution of male-female relations can
continue its development. This means a restructuring of our
present arrangements of where and when men and women
can be gainfully employed while still providing a domestic
support system for their children.

In the restructuring of our society, industry should retain
all the benefits that science has brought us under the banner

of the patriarchal revolt against nature. The restructuring would restore to our technological society the structure of a preindustrial society. Trends in this direction are already evident in Europe. In *Rethink: A Paraprimitive Solution,* Gordon Rattray Taylor goes into considerable detail on pioneering trends in Europe that allow some optimism about the advent of a metatechnological, or what we would call a metaprimitive, society.

Taylor and Rosemary Ruether both agree that this kind of social restructuring is essential and "probably the only type of society compatible with the long-term ecological survival of humanity on earth."

Restructuring our society in terms of men and women sharing equally in our economic productivity and political life will mean a host of changes. With no pretense to being complete or indicating relative importance, the following list is representative of the types of changes we will encounter:

Equalized social-security benefits for married women who work outside the home and those who are housewives.
Adequate retirement benefits for all, including housewives.
Restructured workweek and school schedules for co-ordination of family leisure.
Extensively planned communities for communal child care and other familial and individual support needs.
Lessened emphasis on single-unit homes.
Equalized taxes to eliminate biases in favor of any group, male or female, single or married.
Widowers' benefits under social security and more emphasis on life insurance for women, especially housewives, to provide for loss of their services.
Elimination of employment biases against young married women, mothers, and pregnant women.
Elimination of sex restrictions in all but a very few jobs in which simple physical strength is essential.
Restructured alimony and child support with the possibility of no alimony or the husband's receiving it, and with the

wife's domestic services included in an equitable accounting of the couple's estate.

Changes in our aggressive competitive consumerist capitalism toward community and personal services.

Displacement of outmoded male aggressiveness in economics and politics.

New political structures on all levels from local to federal governments, shifting from patriarchal hierarchical democracy to more flexible communalized republican organizations.

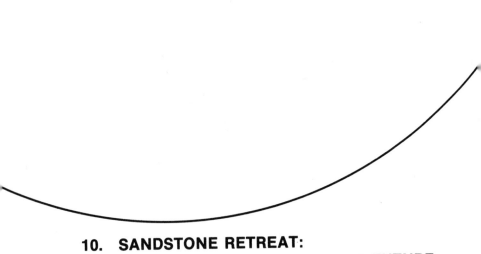

**10. SANDSTONE RETREAT:
ONE ENCLAVE OF THE FUTURE**

By the same token, just as we [should] make it possible for some people to live at the slower pace of the past, we must also make it possible for individuals to experience aspects of their future in advance. Thus, we shall also have to create enclaves of the future.

—ALVIN TOFFLER, *Future Shock*

It should be clear that, in the new society, the emphasis will not be so much on categorizing or labeling of man-woman or sexual relationships, but on the sensitive awareness and enjoyment of distinctions, and the recognition that an awareness of these distinctions has something to do with the outcomes or direction of the relationship.

—HERBERT OTTO, "Man-Woman Relationships in the Society of the Future"

Few people living today will be able to overcome the Hot Sex attitudes and values absorbed since birth. Yet we can hope that more of us will come to appreciate where we are today, and then do something positive about our personal growth and relationships.

Change is never easy. It taxes our mind as we try to understand how we got where we are and then try to rationalize our way back to a new starting point. It taxes our emotional energies as we try to cope with feelings of guilt and shame over our desire to step to the beat of a different drummer. Change is our lifeblood. However, a clear image of where our society seems to be headed helps ease the pains of adaptation and growth. But then theories and hopes have to be given flesh.

If we are to meet the challenges of identity, maturity, and personal growth, if we are to make the most of these opportunities, then we have to be willing not only to shift gears into new thought patterns, but also to channel our energies toward creating small functional enclaves of the future. The task is to create transitional tribal environments to which we can retreat for short periods of time, secure and reassuring environments in which we can learn to relate in more human and intimate ways, transitional environments that allow us to cope with the realities of a new set of behavioral patterns. Visitors to an enclave of the future should be able to return to our patriarchal Hot Sex society with a new perspective and sense of values that will help them continue growing.

In the middle of the last century, fascinating enclaves of the future were sprouting all over the American continent, at the rate of three or four hundred a year. Most of these utopian ventures quickly withered away, lost in the pervasive patriarchal bias of that era. But their very existence created an awareness that human relationships had not reached their zenith in the inflexible Victorian models. They signaled the possibility of a new set of values, but it was a premature rebellion.

During the night of September 21, 1823, Joseph Smith received a heavenly visitor who charged him with leading the Church of Jesus Christ of Latter-day Saints. In their trek across the American continent, the Mormons accepted a venerable but scandalous form of male-female relations, the multilateral relationship of one husband and several wives. Joseph Smith himself entered into thirty-two "celestial marriages," but always as the grand patriarch. John Humphrey Noyes, the founder and leader of the Oneida Community, was equally patriarchal, despite the high position of women in the community and their practice of complex marriage in which all members shared the marital bond and sexual access. At the other end of the scale in sexual attitudes was George Rapp's Harmony Farm, with its strict religious, celibate marriage customs and patriarchal rule. The celibate Shakers achieved true orgiastic release in their ritual dances, but they were more communal and democratic than the members of Harmony Farm. The intellectual communes of Massachusetts, at Hopedale, Fruitlands, and Brook Farm, attracted such notables as Nathaniel Hawthorne and Ralph Waldo Emerson to explore new social structures that included various types of property sharing, nudism, and sexual equality. Short-lived as these enclaves of the future were, they did provide a spark. There was so much patriarchal Hot Sex to cut through that few of these experiments could manage more than a very fuzzy and narrow glimpse of the future. The last few decades of American life have revived the visionary spirit, especially among the youth. The impersonalism of modern technology and the fragmentation of mobile life created the hippie and rural communes, the tribal flower children, all of whom sought a new life based on a return to some natural Eden and a rejection of everything associated with modern technology. Cool Sex values, the rejection of competition, property, and materialism, and the embracing of sense experience and human sexuality in everyday life have emerged in many of these experiments, but so have male chauvinism and sexist roles. Very few people conditioned from birth to all the comforts of modern life can retreat successfully into primitivism. Rural and hippie communes are seldom successful because they reject the progress of human knowledge in toto rather than only in what is inhuman and depersonalizing. These communities are really enclaves more of the past than of the future. But they revitalize some components of our Cool Sex model evident in the attitudes and behavior patterns of past tribal cultures.

More promising in terms of models for the future are the profession-, service-, and church-related communes of middle-aged couples that have sprung up in cities and suburbs. They are often unnoticed by the mass media, but their influence is quite real. Equally anonymous are the isolated but numerous couples who are finding themselves unexpectedly grappling with the challenge of broadening their exclusive relationships into more growth-oriented multilateral networks of varying intensities. It is almost impossible to document these experiences because of their informal nature, yet they are also important. The media, of course, prefer exploiting the shock value of the swinger and consensual-adulterer subcultures. These also create their own enclave of the future, however limited and fragmented it may be. Today's college generation is viewed as unquestionably the most sexually liberated, future-oriented subculture on the American scene. Their dating and courtship patterns, their attitudes toward nonmarital cohabitation, their tribal families in coed dormitories all seem to reflect the dominance of Cool Sex attitudes and values. But when one really probes into their values, as we have done, one begins to question that public image. Underlying their supposed radical values is a substratum of unacknowledged Patrist attitudes. Their premarital behavior is quite apart from their unquestioned traditional monogamous values in marriage. When they accept the institution of marriage, as they usually do in the end, it is with the traditional expectations of their parents and grandparents.

As alternatives to our present culture, each of these subcultures has its distinct value. The problem is that fragmentation and the lack of communication between these subcultures greatly reduce their impact on our mainstream culture.

Studying an effective enclave of the future is a frustrating task in any age, but in today's prefigurative culture it is even more exasperating. The very nature of a prefigurative culture is that it does not have univocal, clearly defined social models for the individual male and female, the dyadic relationship, and the structure and function of the family.

We have discussed this problem with Robert Rimmer, Rustum Roy, and other observers. We have always ended up with some anonymous, isolated pioneering group. One case, however, stands out as an innovative enclave of the future, a fascinating if sometimes puzzling experiment with Cool Sex.

■ *Retreat to the Future*

Bob's introduction to Sandstone came in the fall of 1971 at a conference of scientists and theologians at Kirkridge Retreat in the Pocono Mountains. Rustum Roy, who had organized the conference, introduced Bob to Barbara and John Williamson, the founders of Sandstone. In his early forties, John seems at ease with himself and the world. He has a squarish, open face, intelligent eyes, thinning reddish-blond hair, and a soft Alabama voice that draws one into physical as well as mental intimacy. Trained as an engineer, he worked in the early 1960's for Lockheed Aircraft as a project manager on the design and management of missile-support systems. He left Lockheed to open his own electronics firm and made a small fortune that allowed him to set up Sandstone in 1967. Barbara has a very successful career as an insurance saleswoman.

From early evening, when the conference's work sessions ended, until two or three in the morning that weekend, Barbara and John talked about their experiment. It was difficult and disturbing trying to understand what appeared to be a very radical alternate life style involving communal living, optional nudity, and open sexuality. By the end of the weekend it was clear that we would have to pursue this experiment in more depth.

Two weeks later, Barbara and John Williamson spent a few days with us in Rockaway, which gave us both an opportunity to question them in more depth about Project Synergy, need hierarchies, and value systems, and to raise all our skeptical, practical questions about everyday life at Sandstone. During the next year, Bob's three visits to Sandstone, two of them long weekends, provided the firsthand observations needed to detail our picture of this enclave of the future.

In *Eve's New Rib*, we defined Sandstone as an

intentional or engineered environment which facilitates the formation and evolution of various types of communities among its members. Sandstone simply tries to facilitate human relations and intimacies of all types and intensities within an atmosphere that respects human dignity and individualities. It is a search for the possibilities of what communities might be.

This rather abstract and stilted description still holds, but with our more detailed insights into Hot and Cool Sex, we would like to expand it. Sandstone is an experimental, transitional "tribal environment," an enclave of the future. It is a transitional environment because its members are constantly aware that its function is to provide a Cool Sex tribal milieu in which people can "retreat" from our Hot Sex culture and experience in a nonthreatening environment the diffused sensuality and expanded multilateral relations of varying intensities and intimacies that together characterize our future as a global tribal culture. All the other experiments we know of have been inwardly focused groups, content to do their own thing. Uniquely, Sandstone saw itself as a community concerned with education, or, more exactly, with changing the behavioral patterns and value systems of our society.

Most people find it impossible to cast off their Hot Sex mentality alone. They need support, encouragement, and guidance. In this sense Sandstone is an educational bridge rather than a retreat, as the hippie or many rural communes are. It combines an alternative life style based on Maslow's humanistic psychology and his principles of synergy, or growth reinforcement; a private country club that can vary from hot to cool in its values and behavior; a Cool Sex-oriented retreat; and a sociological research community centered in a half-million-dollar estate with some five hundred members.

The physical setting of Sandstone is ideal. Though people are by far the most vital element in creating an enclave of the future, the physical setting can certainly promote or hinder the group's behavior. For someone whose time is mostly spent in a Hot Sex culture, a dramatic shift in environment can heighten the effectiveness of his retreat to the future.

There is something other-worldly about Sandstone's setting that breaks people out of their usual frame of reference. It embraces fifteen acres of wildly exotic land perched on the virgin crest of Topanga Canyon. Intuitively one senses that Sandstone is built on a whole different set of values and expectations. The vibrations are there as one's eyes reach out from the austere Malibu Mountains around Sandstone, down over Santa Monica Bay, to the endless ocean dotted only by the island of Catalina in the distant haze. The subliminal effect of the physical setting gently breaks down the protective barriers so common in our competitive technological bustle. The physical facilities of Sandstone reinforce the subtle geographic message, offering a variety of moods and environments. Two of these microenvironments are located in the two-story U-shaped ranch house inserted into the sloping mountainside. The upper level is typical of Sandstone's true philosophy: a sensuous, warm relation-oriented setting. A large brick fireplace is flanked by glass doors opening onto a redwood deck, green grass, and sky-blue water. There is a thick golden carpet, and three plush couches in slightly darker honey circle a low glass-topped oak table before the fireplace, the arched cathedral beams highlighted by a massive wrought-iron cartwheeled chandelier. The warmth of natural wood sets the tone in that sixty-by-twenty-foot living area. A small library on human relations, sexuality, psychology, and alternate life styles is located above recessed window seats at one end. The dining room, with a Renaissance carved-oak table, a narrow but cozy kitchen usually populated by more men than women, and two private bedrooms complete the other wing of this microenvironment.

Downstairs is a transitional environment much closer to Hot Sex values. A plush red carpet covers this sixty-by-twenty-foot room, often reinforced by sensuous strobes and rock music. Erotic fantasies are kindled by several giant mattresses, king-sized water beds, and a pool table at one end of the room and, at the other, sliding glass doors hidden by drapes, a bar, and another large room completely carpeted with mattresses.

The patio in the U-shaped alcove outside the living area reflects another set of relational values in the informality of a large barbecue kitchen and sensual water cascading from a fountain into a shallow pool.

Yet another transitional microenvironment is created in the relaxing sensuality of an indoor Olympic-sized pool. A tropical mist from the 92-degree water condenses on redwood beams into gentle barrier-dissolving drops. Several smaller guest cottages complete the pluralistic environment that houses the Sandstone experiment.

John and Barbara Williamson have tried many times to express the essence of what they have attempted to do:

The strength and lasting significance of the Sandstone experience lies in human contact divorced from the cocktail context with all its games and dodges and places to hide. . . . [It is] a new kind of community where a person's mind, body, and being are no longer strangers to each other.

In some respects the varied members of Sandstone are reminiscent of the people who contributed to the Brook Farm community in the last century. They are predominantly achievers, but also concerned with their continued growth as individuals—doctors, actresses, accountants, nurses, students, teachers, business executives, lawyers, writers, explorers, artists. Many, if not the majority, are struggling for a deeper understanding of themselves and their relations with others. Reasons for coming to Sandstone vary greatly, but they all seem to reflect a deep-seated need for a new type of honesty, sharing, and freedom from the artificial.

■ Change Mechanisms

In the unusual design of Sandstone's multienvironments, members are free to do whatever they like in terms of human relationships. The only restrictions are mutuality and respect for the rights of others. The focus has been on two major "change mechanisms"—optional nudity and open sexual expression—specifically chosen because they have proven effective in helping people cope with two prime obstacles to human relations in our Hot Sex culture: possessiveness and jealousy. Tom Hatfield, who spent four years in the Sandstone family, says that the optional nudity makes people much more aware of themselves as physical beings. It also completely changes the level of communication between people, "by eliminating the social-status games of clothes and opening up the often ignored level of nonverbal communications. The defenselessness of nudity inhibits dishonesty. You are what you are, without pretense or surface defense."

The second change mechanism, open and truly optional sexuality, is more radical. Hot Sex obsessions with genital intercourse too often create barriers to real communication outside the marital bond. The lack of in-depth interpersonal relations is probably the most pressing problem in our society. People cannot exist, let alone grow, in a society in which such relationships are severely restricted to those anticipating or already committed in marriage. Sexuality, John Williamson maintains, "can be a barrier to improving relationships, but at the same time it is irrelevant to their ultimate success or failure." So why not bring it out in the open, take away the Hot Sex compulsion to perform, and put sexual intercourse in its proper perspective as one, but not the central, facet in human relationships? If the "sex thing" is blocking or, conversely, overwhelming the relationship, freedom to explore that aspect will let people get on with the realities of their relationship, let them find out whether it was just the passing physical attraction of being turned on or a relationship really worth effort and time.

These change mechanisms are only part of the intriguing facets of Sandstone. The most frightening aspect, however, is its open acceptance of pluralism without pressure to participate or conform. It is frightening for men and women in their thirties, forties, and fifties who have been raised on Hot Sex attitudes and values, but they seem better able to cope with the shift than the young. Tom Hatfield remarked about the college students he had observed at Sandstone over four years: "Emotionality scares the hell out of 'em, intimacy scares them. They talk a good game, and they look a good game, but they can't play the game."

He cited two instances of this youthful reaction to Cool Sex. A boy and two girls from UCLA spent two weeks trying to adjust to Sandstone, hoping to become members of the core family. They finally left, "freaked out by the love and intimacy." Three groups of journalism students from UCLA, Pierce College, and Pasadena City College came up in search of a story. Each group started off their interviews with gusto, went into a trance, and then left muttering something about coming back again to dig deeper into the Sandstone philosophy. None ever returned to finish their story. Perhaps this reaction is a natural outcome of the American myth that life and sexuality are restricted to those under twenty-five or thirty. To recognize the sexuality of people over thirty means recognizing the sexuality of one's parents, and even grandparents—something many Americans are uncomfortable with.

In essence, three levels of involvement contribute to the structure and function of the Sandstone Retreat. Barbara and John Williamson were the backbone of continuity between 1967 and late 1972, when the retreat closed. The family members lived there and handled all the practicalities of the club. In the fall of 1971 and spring of 1972, the family consisted of Barbara and John Williamson, Tom Hatfield, who managed the club, Marty Zitter, who with Sue Bottfeld handled public relations, Jonathon and Bunnie Dana, prime figures in producing a ninety-minute documentary on Sandstone, Janice Smith, and Doug Dingman, the master gourmet chef. This group set the basic tone at Sandstone and offered a flexible ever-evolving pattern for the whole community.

Most of the everyday decisions about Sandstone were made at the Monday-night meetings. Differences of opinion between two parties that could not be ironed out could always be brought before the whole family on Monday night, or, if pressing enough, at a special meeting called by any family member. Sometimes the Monday meetings lasted five minutes, sometimes four or five hours.

The variety of secure, relaxed couples, some married, some paired, who composed a second level of involvement in the retreat probably came the closest to approaching the goals Sandstone valued in terms of a new set of standards. These couples often dropped in on one of the nonparty days, or on a quiet evening. Their social gathering, with its center of activity a buffet dinner and the warm congeniality of the main living area, was on Wednesday night.

Saturday night was the most atypical of Sandstone's philosophy. The change mechanisms and microenvironments were the same, but the tone was much more aggressive. The Saturday-night parties had a Hot Sex swingers' atmosphere more popular with many club members because it was congenial and less demanding in terms of challenging their usual value system and behavior. Tom Hatfield admitted that a "good" Saturday-night party "could literally burn your circuits for weeks." Most of the activity moved quickly to the erotic quarters of the ranch, where one could experience practically any adolescent Hot Sex "candy-store fantasy."

The rationale behind this facet of Sandstone, which appears to be contrary to its philosophy, is both functional and pragmatic. On the functional side, many persons, males especially, get hung up in a maze of aggressive Hot Sex fantasies that prevent them from maturing as sexual persons. With the opportunity to live out this fantasy, about one person in ten learns to move beyond that stage and come to grips with the more real questions of intimacy, fidelity, and responsibility. As the exhilaration of the "candy-store fantasy" wears off, some members find themselves painfully developing a new, deeper consciousness of themselves as sexual persons and exploring ways of relating without being obsessed by sexual intimacy or chained by the reduction of fidelity to exclusive property. The Saturday-night party provides a safe filter through which people can test whether they can handle the demands of a growth-oriented life. On the pragmatic side is the bald reality that without the annual $240-per-couple membership dues, Sandstone would not be financially viable.

■ *Eupsychian Life Styles*

The Sandstone philosophy deeply reflects the humanistic psychology of Abraham Maslow, who believes that every individual must fulfill a hierarchy of needs in order to achieve his fullest potential. Our most basic needs are physiological: nourishment and protection from the elements. With these satisfied, we can be concerned with a comfortable income, job security, reliable health care. Once these needs are met—and most of middle-class America has reached this point—we can devote our real energies to meeting our "metaneeds" for expanded social and interpersonal relationships, self-esteem, and self-actualization. John Williamson has adopted this perspective along with Maslow's undeveloped insights into a synergistic community based on that psychologist's principles of "eupsychian management," and has complemented Maslow's ideas with his own concept of an exotic multilevel memory computer program, using Casyndekan modeling, that can simulate and project the dynamics of a community as it develops.

In the eupsychian community envisioned by Maslow, Peterman, Benedict, and Williamson, synergy, or mutual reinforcement, creates a society whose energies and accomplishments are greater than the simple mathematical sum of those of the individual members. Such a community contrasts strongly with the patriarchal society, which believes in competition and survival of the fittest. Here the people at the bottom spend most of their time struggling to meet their basic physiological and security needs. The people at the top can comfortably spend all their inner energies on self-actualization, interpersonal relations, and personal satisfaction. Unfortunately, they often waste their energy in protecting their position from the realities of competition, or go off into flights of paranoia, as demonstrated by Watergate. The most frustrated people in this pyramid are those in the middle. In an eupsychian community the individual members work together in reinforcement and mutual collaboration. The despair and self-destructive aggression of the ghetto and inner city are transformed into hope and growth, because the community realizes that, in a paraphrase of John Donne, the unsatisfied metaneeds of any group within a community weaken that community and reduce the chances of all its members for reaching their full potential. The prime problem with hierarchies is their tendency to become rigid. This rigidity in turn generates fixed roles that must be filled by forcing people to conform—a tremendous waste of energy that could be better invested in meeting people's needs.

Communications are also a problem in an autocratic pyramid. Decrees descend from above, with little feedback from below. The response of those below tends to become a despairing conditioned reflex, with the threat of violence always in the background. Communications in a synergistic community depend on person-to-person contact undistorted by roles and status.

In terms of simplified social models, the choice seems to lie between the entropic competitiveness and growth-inhibiting roles of an autocratic hierarchical pyramid, on one side, and a flexible, republican, synergistic community support system in which personal growth is maximized, on the other.

As an enclave of the future, Sandstone is unique in both its structure and its goals. Like most ventures, Sandstone has had its successes and its failures. While the data are far from complete, the over-all impression is very favorable. Several studies have been done from the psychiatric, sociological, and anthropological points of view, but only a few have been published. Interviews and tests with representative samples of the more than 8,000 people who have been at Sandstone are being analyzed to find answers to a variety of questions. What brought people to this unique venture? What were the varied effects of this experience? Did they profit from it? How? Was it a damaging experience? How? Why did people drop out of the club or leave the family? How was their human potential affected by Sandstone? These are questions for which only some limited answers are now available.

If Sandstone has radically changed a significant portion of the 8,000 persons for the better, it can be judged a qualified success. The questions are: (1) What is acceptable as a radical change for the better? and (2) What is a significant percentage? At this point, our answer must be an educated approximation: a significant change for the better comprises a noticeable improvement in a person's ability to form fulfilling relationships with other persons, a perceptible adjustment in values from Hot to Cool Sex, greater ease with one's own sexuality and with that of others, a more secure openness to the future and the changes it demands of us, and, finally, an increased ability to achieve peak experiences more often. In terms of significant attitudinal and behavioral changes, estimates suggest that between 10 and 20 per cent of Sandstone's participants would qualify. This may sound insignificant in terms of the numbers affected and those seemingly unchanged by the experience, but in terms of a radical adjustment to a radical new value system, one out of ten constitutes a promising result.

In pointing out some of the main problems and failures in the Sandstone experiment, we do so with constructive concern. Some of the failures obvious in hindsight were undoubtedly not anticipated four or five years ago, when the retreat opened. A few of the problems were insurmountable in terms of practical limitations such as money and time.

One persistent dilemma was a subtle tension between the family and the Saturday-night club members. Tom Hatfield admitted that the "family did not feel very positive about the weekend invasions and parties." Cleaning up after the parties was the unappreciated weekly task of the family.

For the most part, the family remained somewhat aloof from the Saturday-night parties, bored or turned off by the Hot Sex behavior. A critical problem within the family core was a lack of strong, established pair-bond relationships. John and Barbara Williamson stand out in the dynamic strength of their relationship, but practically all the other members joined as single persons. As we observed earlier, most primary relationships have to go through a period of romantic, exclusive, possessive bonding to establish the security and trust essential to an open relationship. John and Barbara maintain that Sandstone may be an ideal environment in which to develop a solid nonneurotic primary relationship. Ideally we might agree, but we are dealing today with people the vast majority of whom are immersed in the neurotic obsessions of our Hot Sex culture. For them the direct approach is often overwhelming. Tom Hatfield admitted as much when he told us that Sandstone is "a very difficult environment to start a primary relationship in. Most of the couples that have lived here haven't taken the time to build a strong primary bond before experimenting outside that bond, so the outside relationships tend to weaken the primary."

The strength of Barbara's and John's primary bond and the fact that they provided all of the half-million-dollar financing and consequently had the final say on all important matters also created a subtle tension. The insecurity of family members struggling with faltering or incipient primary relationships and the newness of the system were compounded by the realities of communal living.

Another problem in maintaining the retreat was limited finances from membership fees. Sometimes, to ease the pressures, couples who really did not fit in with the Sandstone philosophy would be accepted as members. The theory was that if they were a problem, their memberships could always be canceled. But this is a temporary adjustment, not a solution.

The financial limitations finally caught up with Sandstone in late 1972. The retreat was officially closed on December 28 of that year.

■ Project Synergy

One year later the Sandstone family is scattered. Tom Hatfield is using his four years' experience to establish a smaller model of the family and club in Oregon. Marty Zitter and Sue Bottfeld have joined forces with Paul Paige and Theresa Breedlove to reopen the retreat in Topanga in January 1974. Both of these ventures are promising because of the talented and experienced people behind them. But we are somewhat skeptical about whether the basic philosophy and value set that made the original Sandstone so unique can be revitalized.

Barbara and John Williamson, Doug Dingman, and Jonathon and Bunnie Dana are in Montana, looking ahead to creating a "large-scale community project," Project Synergy. John Williamson describes this as "an intentional, multidimensional program . . . somewhat resembling a small, modern community purposely isolated from the larger society yet retaining ready access to [its] transportation, industrial, educational, and recreational facilities." Like Sandstone, it will utilize a physical environment carefully designed to support human needs in such areas as space, privacy, mutual interaction, aesthetics, and variety of experience.

Ideally, Project Synergy "will stabilize in size at approximately one hundred adults, male and female, with established pair-bond relationships. The number of children involved remains a variable and is subject to initial selection processes as well as changing community attitudes and mores."

John Williamson's hope of tying this dynamic experimental community in with a Casyndekan computer model has some interesting and challenging possibilities. However, it is also likely to create definite, perhaps insurmountable, tensions for the community members. No matter how sophisticated the explanation or the sensitivity of the members to the values of computer simulation, no matter how devoted they may be to the principles enunciated by Abraham Maslow, a central problem for Project Synergy will be the subliminal image of Big Brother. Four or five generations from now, Casyndekan computer simulation and projection may not seem as threatening. Nevertheless, there is something about this side of the project that is enticing. Williamson feels that traditional faith in the future, including our religions, has lost most of its motivating force. He sees the Casyndekan simulation, not as some sort of ogre or Big Brother, but, rather, as a "transcendental mechanism in human hands and control." Its function would be to draw us into the future, beyond ourselves and the present, by forecasting a set of probable alternatives to any present situation and allowing us to choose among those alternatives. This computer simulation and projection would constitute a continuous process in developing the eupsychian community. It is possible that even without the feedback and transcendental functions of the computer the potential of a Project Synergy for a hundred adults and their children is worth exploring.

Robert Kaiser, a former editor for *Time* magazine and now with the New York Rand Institute, drew an interesting comparison between John Williamson and Robert Heinlein's Valentine Michael Smith that will help us draw this discussion to a close. In an article in *Penthouse*, "Sandstone—A Love Community," Kaiser says:

Of course, Williamson didn't grow up on Mars, but he grokked the way our sacrosanct sex codes help make people unhappy and, like Smith, he rejected that part of the code which says, "Thou shalt not covet thy neighbor's wife." Like Smith, Williamson has said, "There is no need to covet my wife. Love her. There's no limit to her love, we have everything to gain, and nothing to lose but fear and guilt and hatred and jealousy."

Kaiser asks what will happen to Barbara and John Williamson and their many "water brothers." With our growing tolerance for pluralism and alternate life styles, they are obviously not going to be forced off the earth. Sandstone Retreat is open with new leadership. No one can say for sure at this time whether Project Synergy or some form of it will become a reality, but many people are dedicated to turning the next step beyond Sandstone into reality.

We hope that other experiments will pick up the challenge as our society continues to explore the types of human relations that will prove most functional and rewarding in our emerging tribal culture. But if these are to succeed, the experimenters will have to do a lot of preparation and planning to avoid the mistakes and limitations of past experiences. Most essential will be satisfying the need for a basic flexible process, philosophy, and value system. Just such a value system is what made Sandstone unique and so important sociologically. Duplicating Sandstone's mechanisms and behavioral patterns might prove interesting, but without a life-giving philosophy such an experiment would have little long-term impact.

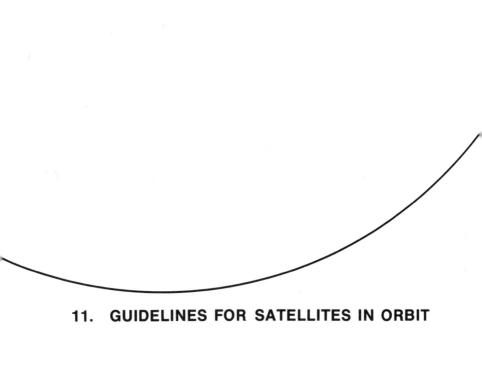

11. GUIDELINES FOR SATELLITES IN ORBIT

Most of the trouble in marriages I have worked with stems from the enormous burden that some marriages carry in pretending to be the total solution to a man or woman's longing for intimacy. Marriages break under that burden. It may be time we began to unburden marriage of the necessity of meeting all an individual's needs for intimacy. It may be time we openly confessed what we all know secretly, that many persons need a variety of relationships in order to find stimulation to grow and develop fully as persons.
—THE REVEREND RAYMOND LAWRENCE, "Toward a More Flexible Monogamy"

Just as by becoming more yourself you can relate more fully to other people, so by loving nonpossessively can you become closer than ever to your mate. And because you are closer than ever to your mate, because the love between you is constantly expanding, so too is it possible for you to include others more easily within the widening circle of your love.
—NENA O'NEILL AND GEORGE O'NEILL, *Open Marriage*

We have often asked our audiences a series of questions when introducing our discussion of Hot and Cool Sex and satellite relations. "Picture a typical middle-class housewife on a shopping expedition. In the same shopping mall, picture a male neighbor, married or single, of about the same age. At noon, both happen to be entering the same uncrowded restaurant. If you were that man or woman, would you sit alone, or would you spontaneously suggest sharing a table?"

More often than not three-quarters of our audiences admit they would eat alone, due to our common habit of equating the association of married people with adults of the opposite sex in a one-to-one situation with genital sex. To emphasize our point, let's ask some variations on this theme:

Would you feel free to go to a concert with a friend of the opposite sex if your spouse did not want to go and said he or she genuinely would prefer to stay home?

Would you feel free, especially as a married woman, to go on a vacation alone with a friend? Would it make any difference if that friend were of the same or the opposite sex? Why?

How would you react if your spouse commented on his or her reaction to some friend along lines that clearly indicated he or she found that person exceptionally attractive and sexy? Would you feel free to make a comment like this to your spouse? And how would your spouse take it?

As a working person, would you feel free to go to dinner and a show with a co-worker of the opposite sex? As a housewife, would you feel free to invite a male friend out to dinner and a show while your husband cooked dinner and cared for the children at home?

The responses to these various questions often reveal the double standard. What is permissible, or at least tolerated, for the male is often forbidden for the woman, the wife, the mother. Men will often be more receptive to a certain freedom for their wives if they feel that the wife's male companion is "safe." As one woman put it, "Toads— physically unattractive and blah men—or cultured homosexuals make safe companions for married women in the middle and upper classes of our society."

There is no denying the Hot Sex obsession of our culture. It permeates the air we breathe, coloring every discussion and every decision on male-female relationships.

■ *Are Satellites Necessary?*

Consequently, we have to give a two-faced answer to a basic question: Can you have an Open Marriage and still have a sexually exclusive relationship?

Our answer is yes.

At the same time, we are firmly convinced that in one real sense this combination is impossible. As long as a man or woman has not accepted the possibility of a satellite relationship involving genital relations for his or her spouse, lingering suspicions about the spouse's friends of the opposite sex cannot be avoided. If you want an open, trusting marriage, you must accept *emotionally and intellectually* the possibility of your spouse's entering into a satellite relationship of which sexual expression is a real part. Without open trust, married friends will continue their androgynous existence as inseparable male-female "twin-packs."

However, given this open trust and a Cool Sex attitude toward fidelity, there is no reason to rule out the possibility of a lifelong sexually exclusive relationship. The crucial difference here is that the couple who have accepted emotionally and intellectually the possibility of a sexual relationship outside the marriage have traded the static Hot Sex expectation of fidelity for the dynamic value of fidelity as a commitment based on loving concern and responsibility. This shift in values is the key to an entirely different way of life.

The majority of couples in Open Marriages will probably not be sexually exclusive. Most couples in Open Marriages will be sexually exclusive most of the time, although both partners will enjoy the enrichment of several satellite relationships far more intimate and rewarding than the friendships presently acceptable. Once satellite relationships are socially accepted as a way of relating that does not necessarily threaten the marriage, the potential for sexual intimacy will lose much of its allure and all of its compulsive performance motives. As Peterman stressed, in "Towards Interpersonal Fulfillment in an Eupsychian Culture":

Often the interpersonal needs people are attempting to meet in relationships outside of marriage are only tangentially related to sexual satisfaction. However, our society now permits only limited interaction in public between the husband from one couple and the wife from another, particularly if spouses are absent. Thus, the real needs—which may in fact be highly "innocent" ones, and which could be acceptably satisfied between same-sex friends in public—are pushed into the background. The relationship develops in secret, it takes on the character of an "affair," and people do what is expected or predicted of them under such conditions [by our Hot Sex expectations].

Some may wonder why we have felt a need to coin a new expression like "satellite relationship" to describe what appears to be simply a good friendship. Actually, we are describing a new concept. The word "friendship" in its old context is very specific about boundaries and limitations. Friends of the same sex are bound by very minimal restrictions. But friends of the opposite sex, particularly when married, are hedged in by a wide variety of restrictions, especially in the area of physical communication. Needless to say, we are not talking here only about sexual intimacy. Our prime concerns are the restrictions placed on married friends of the opposite sex in the area of emotional attachment, emotional expression, and touching. Others have felt a similar need for a new label. Peterman, for instance, has struggled with "clusters," "networks," "constellations," for want of better labels. Maslow suggested "intimacy group," and the Roys "comarital relationship."

Whatever the label, we are talking about a new, more open relationship between people. The Roys, with the help of the Reverend William Genné, a Methodist minister and director of Family Life Services for the National Council of Churches, defined comarital as "without the pejorative connotation of the term extramarital, any man-woman relationship, and/or sexual expression thereof, which exists alongside and in addition to a marriage relationship. Such relationships are basically not competitive with the marital relationship; they may have a neutral or even positive effect on it."

The concept of satellite relationships shatters the ego-

tisme à deux that characterizes traditional monogamy. The Roys struck home when they claimed that *"the first essential step in the evolution of monogamy is the recovery of the role of the community in our lives* [italics added].'' Our technological society has destroyed the sense of human community. It has created a wasteland filled with elbow-bumping nomads who know few people in an intimate way outside their immediate families. The more complex and highly developed a society is, the Roys maintain, the weaker the channels of communication. Technology has forced us to turn to the family as a last resource for human communications, but the nuclear family cannot bear this responsibility. Two human beings cannot stand alone against the world, valiantly proclaiming their ability to meet each other's emotional and sexual needs.

"Most of us," as the Roys observe, "are many-sided polyhedra needing several people to reflect back to ourselves the different portions of our personality.''

In this broad context of emotional support and varied needs, we would like to sketch our guidelines, not rules, for good satellite relationships. They deal with a new kind of interpersonal relationship based on a new set of values. A sexual intimacy is not an essential part of this relationship, though its possibility must be intellectually and emotionally accepted.

■ *Self-identity*

Our goal is to fulfill our own process of becoming persons by uniting with others. But to be united, we must first be fully ourselves, in marriage or out of marriage, in friendships of any depth. Someone who finds his or her personal identity primarily in a role as husband, wife, mother, or daddy's good little girl, or in being a pretty young woman or a mamma's boy, will be unable to handle the responsibilities of a satellite or multilateral relationship. To handle any kind of multilateral relationship, one must to some extent be self-motivated, self-actualizing. If you find your sole identity in your relationship with others or in filling some social role, you will find it disconcerting to be alone and difficult to enjoy being alone. The lack of self-identity carries over into the initial decision making about entering an extramarital relationship. In his counseling experiences, Raymond Lawrence, an Episcopal priest at the Texas Medical Center, has found it common for people to decide against an extramarital relationship simply because they want to be good in the eyes of their parents and society. On the other hand, a great many people get into affairs because they want to rebel against authority.

To be valuable and positive, a satellite relationship requires maturity and self-identity.

■ *A Basically Healthy, Committed Primary Relationship*

Without a serious, basic commitment to a marriage in spite of its shortcomings and defects, any kind of relationship with another person of the opposite sex beyond the most superficial is risky for the marriage. Whether or not it involves sexual intimacy, a satellite relationship can succeed only when a committed primary relationship gives it perspective.

Single people in open satellite relations must have a similar commitment to their single way of life. Tom Hatfield commented on the serious problems members of the Sandstone family ran into when they tried to develop multilateral relationships before they had established firm primary relations:

Marty was having a little trouble handling the whole thing of nonexclusivity because he and Sue hadn't been together long enough to really form much of a relationship. There has to be a period at the beginning of any relationship where the two people are totally monogamous. This can last for any length of time, depending on the two people, but if either of them goes outside the relationship before that level of trust is achieved, it can be very destructive to that pair bond.

Without a firm, committed primary relationship, there is no real trust. Without a firm, committed primary relationship that accepts the natural faults and limitations of the individuals involved, a satellite relationship will ferment comparisons and the urge to try to change the spouse's behavior to match the more suitable characteristic of the satellite that first attracted one.

A healthy committed relationship, however, does not have to be "exclusive and total," either emotionally or sexually. The "exclusive and total" ideal places a tremendous burden of responsibility on the individual. It is the nonexclusive, open trust of a committed primary relationship that alone can incorporate a satellite or multilateral relationship.

■ *A Real Self-image*

To handle a satellite relationship, you must realize and accept the fact that all relationships are partial and limited because we are finite, limited creatures. Once you accept this fact, you will not feel guilty if you cannot satisfy all the needs of your spouse. To match two individuals, often from different backgrounds, so perfectly that they will never think of looking outside their pair relationship is impossible. A realistic self-image accepts this, even though it means that both you and your spouse can expect to fulfill some of your needs occasionally outside your primary relations. A realistic self-image is the basic reason increasing numbers of married persons are turning to Open Marriage and satellite relationships.

■ *Authenticity*

A satellite relationship, to borrow the phrase of the German Redemptorist theologian C. Jaime Snoek, should be "at the service of true, personalizing communications." A satellite relationship should exist because two persons find in it a mutual fulfillment that enriches their personal growth. One should not enter into a satellite relationship to improve a marriage, even though a good satellite relation can strengthen a basically sound marriage. Satellite relationships should not be based on subconscious ulterior motives.

Some Biblical scholars have touched on this point indirectly by suggesting that Jesus' statement "he who looks after a woman in lust has already committed adultery" has been commonly misinterpreted by ignoring the key word: lust. Their interpretation is that any man or woman who uses and exploits another person for his or her own sexual pleasure or ulterior motives is treating that person as an object. This, and not the act of sexual intercourse, constitutes the sinfulness and inhumanity of adultery.

Authenticity in an extramarital relationship, according to Raymond Lawrence, means that the relation meets needs that are not being met by one's spouse. These needs may be due to the understandable shortcomings of the spouse. But they can also be due to the realities of today's family ecosystem and our growing need for variety and for the rejuvenating stimulation that curiosity, adventure, and novelty can bring to a relationship. This is not to deny the fact that an important part of maturity is learning to tolerate the frustration of certain unmet needs.

Men can use an affair as a power play. Men with low self-esteem or failing virility will use it to build their egos or compensate for their flagging masculinity, and neurotic megalomaniacs will use it to compete with the woman's husband. A man will even persuade his lover to have a child to prove her love and his own power to impregnate and subject the female.

Women use affairs equally well as power plays, such as getting pregnant by a lover at a time the husband knows he could not possibly be the father. Not infrequently a wife will deliberately start an affair to even the score with her husband or embarrass him professionally. Sometimes, of course, she is anxious to affirm her continued attractiveness as a woman.

The knowledge of such motives is the basis for the intuitive reaction of many men and women in Open Marriages to the possibility of their spouses' becoming involved with certain people. We have talked with many husbands and wives who have experienced the reaction Tom Hatfield labels a "jealousy of selectivity." Many people say that they do not object to their spouses' having satellite relationships. But they do object to "this woman" or "that man." Often this reaction is not really jealousy, but, rather, an intuitive reaction on the part of a trusting open spouse who senses that the third person is predatory. A wife will bristle if she senses or thinks that a woman is using her husband because the other woman's marriage is faltering or because she is single and looking for a mate. Predatory men and women, single or married, will invariably turn a satellite relationship into a disastrous battleground.

Authenticity also means an acceptance of a satellite relationship as secondary and by its nature subsidiary to the primary bonds either or both may have. Authenticity demands that all parties involved respect and value the primary relationships and other existing relationships, so that the commitment and fidelity of the subordinate relationship will not conflict with those of the primary and other relationships.

■ *Ability to Handle the Loss of Innocence*

Entering a satellite relationship means transgressing the traditional mores of our monogamous culture that condemn extramarital relations. For a religious person, it means going against patent official church teachings. Even for those who profess to be free of any church, there is often lingering subliminal conditioning that can create guilt.

Some responsible theologians are cautiously discussing the possibility that an extramarital relationship involving sex may be part of our Christian commitment and within the covenant announced by Jesus, as, for instance, in the work document of the United Presbyterian Church in the U.S.A.

This may provide psychological and intellectual support for someone's personal decision, and help him realize that he is not necessarily rationalizing or simply indulging a whim or fantasy. But a person who cannot accept the responsibility of his own conscience will not be able to handle the guilt associated with a satellite relationship.

A parallel we have encountered many times on the Roman Catholic scene may clarify this point. Countless theologians and the majority opinion of the papal commission on birth control hold that Catholics may use contraceptives, yet the Pope has said otherwise. Many Catholic women are convinced in their own consciences of the moral righteousness of contraceptives and of the responsibility they have to use them. They and their husbands agree. And everything is fine until some relative casually remarks that their youngest is three and they are not expecting yet. Then the woman begins to feel guilty about not feeling guilty. The same pattern can develop in a satellite relationship: a person begins to feel guilty about not feeling guilty regarding a relationship he or she is convinced is moral and good despite its violation of traditional mores.

Many spouses cannot handle their subconscious guilt in an affair. A husband "accidentally" leaves a motel bill or an incriminating note in his pocket, or pays for a motel room for two with a credit card. Sometimes he will simply confess the affair to the innocent spouse. Subconsciously the motive may be an attempt to regain lost innocence. Confess, be punished and forgiven by your innocent spouse, and once again enjoy the sweet innocence of a child.

■ *Fidelity*

In a satellite relationship there must be a real feeling of fidelity, not in the sense of sexual exclusivity, but in the authentic Biblical meaning of steadfast loving concern.

"Loving concern," according to the Jesuit moralist Thomas Wassmer, is essential to any moral human relationship, marital or otherwise. "I would not call an act adultery (hence unfaithful) if it's an act done with loving concern."

Rustum and Della Roy pick up this same Biblical theme in their book *Honest Sex.* "It is utterly ridiculous to say on the one hand, 'Greater love hath no man than this, that he lay down his life for his friends,' and to assert immediately that it is impossible and unnatural for a man (or woman) to agree to share his (or her) spouse with another. We are claiming then that no black-and-white case can be made against sexual intimacies (including coitus) between persons not married to each other."

In a controversial milestone study, *Sexuality and the Human Community,* adopted by the general assembly of the United Presbyterian Church in the U.S.A. in May 1970, the covenant basis of fidelity in all human relations was stressed in a context directly applicable to the idea that satellite and multilateral relationships can complement and reinforce a Christian marriage:

We regard as contrary to the covenant all those actions which destroy community and cause persons to lose hope, to erode their practical confidence in the providence of God, and to lose respect for their own integrity as persons. Clearly, such actions are not susceptible of being catalogued, for sexual gestures which may in one instance cause deep guilt and shame, whether warranted or not, may in another context be vehicles of celebrating a joyous and creative communion between persons.

By the same token, those sexual expressions which build up communion between persons, establish a hopeful outlook on the future, minister in a healing way to the fears, hurts and anxieties of persons and confirm to them the fact that they are truly loved, are actions which can confirm the covenant Jesus announced.

Interpersonal relationships should enhance rather than limit the spiritual freedom of the individuals in-

volved. They should be vehicles of expressing that love
which is commended in the New Testament—a compas-
sionate and consistent concern for the well-being of the
other. They should provide for the upbuilding of the creative potential of persons who are called to the task of
stewardship of God's world. They should occasion that
joy in his situation which is one of man's chief means of
glorifying his Creator. They should open to persons that
flow of grace which will enable them to bear their burdens without despair.

"A faithful affair," Raymond Lawrence maintains, "is
one engaged in for its own sake, where one seeks primarily
neither to hurt nor to please any other person, and where the
only significant agenda is the intimate participation in the
existence and being of another person." Fidelity in a satellite
relationship embraces the uniqueness of the persons involved, the uniqueness of the relationship and all its limitations.

■ Noncompetitive and Nonpossessive

The traditional extramarital affair is driven by a compulsion
to possess the lover or mistress. The relationship is typically
competitive and often predatory, because in our culture one
intimate relationship automatically excludes all others. In the
Hot Sex affair, there is a compulsion to multiply contacts
and love-making as if numbers can substitute for the quality
of a relationship.

The comarital relationship, on the other hand, is not obsessed with sexual intercourse or with multiplying such experiences merely for the illusion of security this gives. The
comarital relationship, like the Open Marriage, celebrates
the relationship that exists today, seeking to make it a peak
experience for all. A husband often has to fight culture-in-
duced jealousy of his satellite's other intimate relationships.
He not only tries to accept them, but to encourage them as

well. The same holds true for a wife, and the satellite must combat the tendency to be jealous of his or her partner's primary relationship. The partialities of a satellite relationship are not easy, though they can be rewarding when they add to the rewards of a less partial but likewise incomplete primary relationship.

■ Responsibility

Since we are a society that still maintains the myth of marital togetherness, anyone who decides to transgress should be sensitive to the side effects of such an act. Pioneers should be discreet. Besides having the courage of one's convictions, one must be sensitive to the community values and not advertise unnecessarily one's decision not to accept those values. Rustum and Della Roy speak of "other-centeredness," a concern for all the others who will be affected by satellite relationships, especially if they involve sexual intimacy. They maintain that consideration of any children involved "must be front and center in reaching decisions on any such matters."

If the satellite relationships involve sexual intercourse, there is also a responsibility to take proper precautions against pregnancy. The second of Alex Comfort's two basic commandments is "Thou shalt not under any circumstances negligently risk producing an unwanted child."

■ Honesty, Openness, and Trust

Open, honest communications are the basis of any relationship, and especially of multilateral relationship. Satellite relationships constantly evolve in content, depth, and duration. The primary relationships also evolve constantly because they are open ended. Without honest, open, trusting communications this intimate network is bound to collapse. Honesty provides a helpful check on the authenticity of our motives and a safeguard against getting involved as an unsuspecting prey. It also eases the pain of emotional adjustment as one becomes accustomed to expanded relationships and an open primary bond. Frank and honest dialogue strengthens all the bonds, particularly when a satellite relationship has sexual potential. Married couples interested in an Open Marriage should discuss the possibility ahead of time. They may decide against it, or they may find their earlier objections fading with candid dialogue. Still others may conclude that satellite relationships that include sexual expression are both necessary and beautiful.

Few middle-aged couples today entered marriage with any idea that their relationship might not be sexually exclusive. It is not uncommon for such couples to find themselves suddenly confronted with a fairly intense relationship and having been unaware that it was developing. The illusion of togetherness is then shattered with apocalyptic swiftness. The best way to handle such a situation may be to attempt to develop a gradual retroactive openness, starting with the crisis at hand and edging back in time psychologically to explore the roots of the relationship. This inevitably means much tension and anxiety, and requires a lot of sensitive acceptance without immediately pressing for unqualified assent.

In his courageous attempt to analyze his experiences in pastoral counseling of couples grappling with multilateral relationships, Raymond Lawrence has suggested two invaluable insights touching on the issue of communications:

A common fallacy in marriage folklore is that real intimacy means full disclosure of one's thoughts, feelings and actions. I contend that an attempt at total openness is not a true form of intimacy. It is rather a naïve form of dependency. Real intimacy is experienced in the rhythmical movement toward and away from another person. Real intimacy is experienced only when persons have the capacity and wisdom both to give and to withhold, both to move toward and to move away from, both to be close and to be distant. One who cannot be distant destroys the value of his being close. One who cannot be close negates the value of his distance.

Picking up a thread from this insight, Lawrence concludes that total openness about the details of a satellite relationship, especially when this involves sexual expression, may not be an honest form of communication, but, rather, an indirect seeking of approval for one's behavior. "I have found it to be almost invariably true that married persons do not want to hear any of the details of the exploits of their spouses with a third party." One of the limitations of satellite relations is that such experiences often do not lend themselves to full sharing with one's spouse.

■ *Gradualness*

A gradual adjustment to more intimate levels of communication makes it easier for us to meet the challenges of handling multilateral relationships, and allows step-by-step adjustments in our primary relationships without forcing the issue.

And yet this gradual approach is not always practical in our mobile society. Our pace often eliminates the leisure traditionally allowed in developing friendships. As Peterman has eloquently argued, one of the most desperate needs of our society is a way to teach people to communicate authentically and intimately from the start, without the games of social conventions: "Learning to form a budding friendship in a couple of hours of intense and open communication can be a peak experience if you are used to spending weeks or months in getting to the same place in a relationship."

The ten guidelines for satellite relationships just discussed sum up the essential lessons we have found in our study of satellite relations and Open Marriages. They *are* guidelines, not a neat recipe to be followed with mechanical precision. They express what we are convinced is of supreme value in human relations: a commitment to ourselves and to humankind that is rooted in the transcendent, a commitment to become more fully human.

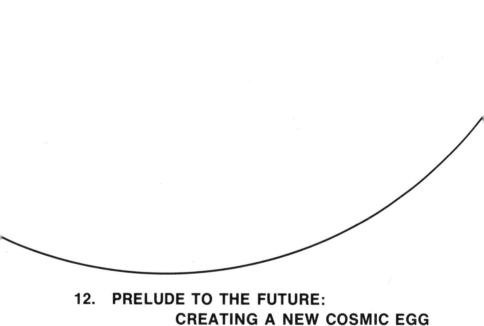

12. PRELUDE TO THE FUTURE:
       CREATING A NEW COSMIC EGG

How will the man of tomorrow live his sexual life? Will he have won greater inner freedom? Will he have destroyed the tyranny of genitality and replaced it by a more discrete form of eroticism, more widespread, more communicative, permeating all human relationships?
—C. JAIME SNOEK, "Marriage and the Institutionalization of Sexual Relations"

A Biblical proverb assures us that without vision, a sense of purpose, an image of our future, we will perish as a society, as a culture, and as individuals.

We have tried to present in this book an objective picture of the past and present in human relationships, along with our own subjective but carefully tested image of the future. If you do not agree with our forecast of a Cool Sex future, we hope you will accept our challenge and develop your own image of the future. No one can infallibly predict what form the relationships between men and women will take, or how they themselves would react and relate if they were to meet fully all their needs in open primary bonds and a variety of satellite relations. The majority of people today still exist within single long-term exclusive relationships. To achieve a more lasting change in our sexual attitudes, our entire value system will have to undergo readjustment. We will have to create, on the social institutional level, eupsychian communities that allow and promote truly nonpossessive, synergistic love.

This is our projection, and we find it fascinating to imagine such a society coming into being in the near future.

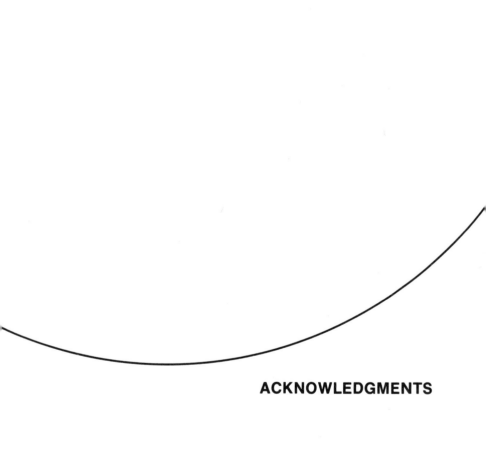

ACKNOWLEDGMENTS

Every book is the product of a variety of coauthors, each of whom contributes some small or large piece to the final volume. Behind *Hot & Cool Sex* are dozens of our friends and acquaintances who helped with bits of essential information, missing links in our analysis, encouragement and reinforcement, criticisms and suggestions. In many ways this book is also their book, though their names do not appear on the jacket or title page with ours.

With the wide range of topics we have had to explore and analyze, we are very grateful that we could call on the critical assistance of Robert H. Rimmer, author of *The Harrad Experiment,* who also introduces our book; Nena O'Neill and George O'Neill, authors of *Open Marriage;* Rustum and Della Roy, of Pennsylvania State University; Rosemary Radford Ruether, of Howard University; Nell Morton, professor emeritus, Drew University School of Theology; James Nagle, geneticist at Drew University; Drew Christianson, of Yale Divinity School and *Theological Studies;* Ivan Huber, geneticist-entomologist at Fairleigh Dickinson University; Roger Johnson, psychologist at Ramapo College, in New Jersey; the Reverend Cornelius van der Poel, now in Guam; Barbara and John Williamson, founders of the Sandstone Retreat, and other members of that community, especially Tom Hatfield and Marty Zitter; and, finally, Professor Alex Comfort, of the University of London.

Our special appreciation goes to the unnamed friends who shared their personal experiences with us so that we could offer examples and reactions drawn from life, rather than just a theoretical analysis. Still other friends helped us with their careful criticism of our rough drafts. These included the Reverend John D. Keister, chaplain at Roanoke College, Dee Keister, Cathy Patla, Mary Kamienski, Barbara and John Williamson, of Sandstone, Miriam Glick, Lela Rames, Eleni Lawrence and the Reverend Raymond Lawrence in Houston, Ronald Gresko, Richard and Dorothy Grandi, and Roger Johnson.

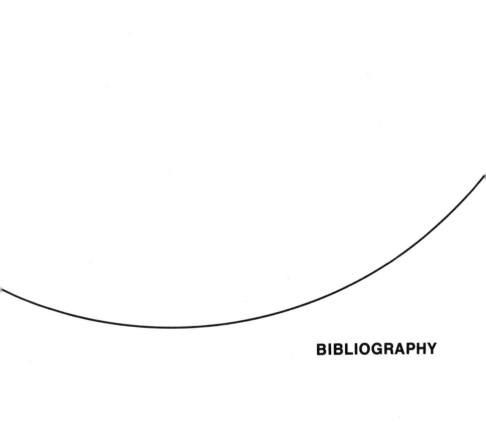

BIBLIOGRAPHY

In the following list, three asterisks after an item indicate essential reading for those who would like to delve more deeply into the various topics we discuss in this book. A double asterisk designates valuable reading in the same context. A single asterisk marks books and articles that have helpful insights but are for the most part peripheral to our interests here. No asterisk indicates material we consulted for background information and insights.

Andreas, Carol. *Sex and Caste in America.* Englewood Cliffs, N.J.: Prentice-Hall, 1971.

Ardrey, Robert. *The Territorial Imperative.* New York: Atheneum, 1966.*

Aries, Philippe. *Centuries of Childhood: A Social History of Family Life.* New York: Random House, 1962.**

Arndt, Karl. *George Rapp's Harmony Society: 1785–1847.* Rutherford, N.J.: Fairleigh Dickinson University Press, 1972.

————. *George Rapp's Successors and Material Heirs: 1847–1916.* Rutherford, N.J.: Fairleigh Dickinson University Press, 1972.

Bach, George, and Deutsch, Ronald. *Pairing.* New York: Avon, 1971.

Baguedor, Eve. "Is Anyone Faithful Anymore?" *McCall's,* February 1973.*

Bartel, Gilbert. *Group Sex.* New York: Peter H. Wyden, Inc., 1971.**

Bell, Robert. *Premarital Sex in a Changing Society.* Englewood Cliffs, N.J.: Prentice-Hall, 1966.*

Belliveau, Fred, and Richter, Lin. *Understanding Human Sexual Inadequacy.* New York: Bantam, 1970.

Bernard, Jessie. *The Future of Marriage.* New York: Macmillan, 1971.***

————. *The Sex Game.* Englewood Cliffs, N.J.: Prentice-Hall, 1968.**

Berne, Eric. *Sex in Human Loving.* New York: Simon and Schuster, 1970.

Binstock, Jeanne. "Motherhood: An Occupation Facing Decline." *The Futurist,* June 1972.*

Birdwhistell, Ray. "The American Family: Some Perspectives." *Psychiatry* 29 (1966):203–212.*

Blenkinsopp, Joseph. *Sexuality and the Christian Tradition.* Dayton, Ohio: Pflaum, 1969.*

Boguslaw, Robert. *The New Utopians: A Study of System Design and Social Change.* Englewood Cliffs, N.J.: Prentice-Hall, 1968.*

Borowitz, Eugene. *Choosing a Sex Ethic: A Jewish Inquiry.* New York: Schocken, 1970.*

Boylan, Brian. *Infidelity.* Englewood Cliffs, N.J.: Prentice-Hall, 1971.

Brent, Iris. *Swinger's Diary.* New York: Pinnacle, 1973.*

Brothers, Joyce. "Will Liberalized Sex Kill Romantic Love?" *Good Housekeeping,* June 1971.*

Brown, Norman. *Life Against Death: The Psychoanalytical Meaning of History.* New York: Random House, 1959.**

———. *Love's Body.* New York: Random House, 1966.**

Buchen, Irving, ed. *The Perverse Imagination: Sexuality and Literary Culture.* New York: New York University Press, 1970.*

Calhoun, Arthur. *A Social History of the American Family from Colonial Times to the Present.* 3 vols. 1919. Reprint. New York: Barnes and Noble, 1960.**

Campbell, Richard. "Sex as an Intimate Communicative Act in the Decades Ahead." *Journal of Home Economics,* November 1970.*

Carden, Maren. *Oneida: Utopian Community to Modern Corporation.* New York: Harper and Row, 1969.*

Clanton, Gordon. "The Contemporary Experience of Adultery: Bob & Carol & Updike & Rimmer." In Roger Libby and Robert Whitehurst, eds., *Renovating Marriage: Toward New Sexual Life Styles.***

Cole, William. *Sex and Love in the Bible.* New York: Association Press, 1959.**

Comfort, Alex. "Communications May Be Odorous." *New Scientists and Science Journal,* February 25, 1971.**

———. *The Joy of Sex.* New York: Crown, 1972.***

———. "The Likelihood of Human Pheromones." *Nature* (London), April 16, 1971.**

———. *The Nature of Human Nature.* New York: Harper and Row, 1967.*

———. *Sex in Society.* London: Duckworth, 1963; New York: Citadel, 1966.*

———. "Sexuality in a Zero Growth Society." *Center Report,* Center for the Study of Democratic Institutions, December 1972.***

Conover, Patrick. "The Potential for an Alternate Society." *The Futurist,* June 1973.*

Constantine, Larry, and Constantine, Joan. *Group Marriage: A Study of Contemporary Multilateral Marriage.* New York: Macmillan, 1973.**

Davids, Leo. "New Family Norms." In Robert T. and Anna K. Francoeur, eds., *The Future of Sexual Relations.* Englewood Cliffs, N.J.: Prentice-Hall, 1974.

———. "North American Marriage: 1990." *The Futurist,* October 1971.*

DeCoster, David. "The New Morality." *Journal of College Student Personnel,* July 1970.

Eggers, Oscar. "Synergamous Marriage: An Answer to Monotonous Monogamy." *The Futurist,* April 1973.*

Erikson, Erik. *Childhood and Society.* rev. ed. New York: Norton, 1964.**

———. *Insight and Responsibility.* New York: Norton, 1964.*

Etkins, W., and Freedman, D. G. *Social Behavior from Fish to Man.* Chicago: Chicago University Press, 1964.

Fast, Julius. *Body Language.* New York: Evans, 1970.*

———. *The Incompatibility of Men and Women and How to Overcome It.* New York: Avon, 1972.

Ferderber, Skip. "Sandstone: Closeup of a Unique Lifestyle." *Los Angeles Times,* April 6, 1972, part 7.*

Ferm, Deane. *Responsible Sexuality—Now.* New York: Seabury, 1971.*

Firestone, Shulamith. *The Dialectic of Sex: The Case for the Feminist Revolution.* New York: Morrow, 1970.**

Fisher, Alan. "Effects of Stimulus Variation on Sexual Satiation in the Male Rat." *Journal of Comparative and Physiological Psychology* 55 (1962):614–620.*

Fitzgerald, George. *Communes: Their Goals, Hopes, Problems.* New York: Paulist-Newman, 1971.*

Ford, Clellan, and Beach, Frank. *Patterns of Sexual Behavior.* New York: Harper and Row, 1951.***

Fowler, Harry. "Variation in Incentive Stimulus and Sexual Behavior in the Male Rat." *Journal of Comparative and Physiological Psychology* 54 (1961):68–71.*

Framo, James, et al. "How Does an Affair Affect a Marriage?" *Sexual Behavior,* September 1972.**

Francoeur, Robert T. "Conflict and Cooperation in the Collectivisation of Man." In G. Browning et al., eds., *Teilhard de Chardin: In Quest of the Perfection of Man.* Rutherford, N.J.: Fairleigh Dickinson University Press, 1973.

————. *Eve's New Rib: Twenty Faces of Sex, Marriage, and Family.* New York: Harcourt Brace Jovanovich, 1972; Dell, 1973; London: MacGibbon and Kee, 1972.***

————. "Images of the Future: Human Hood and Human Relations." *The Humanist,* December 1973.*

————. *Utopian Motherhood: New Trends in Human Reproduction.* New York: Doubleday, 1970; Cranbury, N.J.: A. S. Barnes Perpetua Books, 1973; London: Allen and Unwyn, 1971.***

Francoeur, Robert T., and Francoeur, Anna K. "Hot and Cool Sex: Fidelity in Marriage." In Roger Libby and Robert Whitehurst, eds., *Renovating Marriage: Toward New Sexual Life Styles.***

————. eds. *The Future of Sexual Relations.* Englewood Cliffs, N.J.: Prentice-Hall, 1974.

Friedan, Betty. *The Feminine Mystique.* New York: Norton, 1963.**

Fromm, Erich. *The Art of Loving.* New York: Harper and Row, 1956.*

Gittelson, Natalie. *The Erotic Life of the American Wife.* New York: Delacorte, 1972.*

Gordon, Caroline. *The Beginner's Guide to Group Sex.*
New York: Drake, 1973.*

Greer, Germaine. *The Female Eunuch.* New York: McGraw-
Hill, 1971.**

"Group Marriage and 'Intimate Networks': Some Alternatives
to Communes." *The Futurist,* June 1973.*

Grunt, J. A., and Young, W. C. "Psychological Modification
of Fatigue Following Orgasm (Ejaculation) in the Male
Guinea Pig." *Journal of Comparative and Physiological Psychology* 45 (1952):508–510.*

Hardin, M. Esther. *Woman's Mysteries: Ancient and Modern.*
New York: Bantam, 1973.**

Hart, Harold, et al., eds. *Marriage: For and Against.* New
York: Hart, 1971.**

Harvey, Will. *How to Find and Fascinate a Mistress: And Survive in Spite of It All.* San Francisco: Montgomery
Street Press, 1971.

Haughton, Rosemary. *Love.* London: Watts, 1970.*

———. *The Mystery of Sexuality.* New York: Paulist-Newman,
1972.**

Heinlein, Robert. *Stranger in a Strange Land.* New York:
Berkley, 1968.**

Herrigan, Jackie, and Herrigan, Jeff. *Loving Free.* New York:
Grosset and Dunlap, 1973.

Hunt, Morton. *The Affair: A Portrait of Extra-marital Love in
Contemporary America.* New York: New American Library, 1973.***

———. "Forsaking All Others . . ." *Woman's Day,* May
1973.**

———. *The Natural History of Love.* New York: Alfred A.
Knopf, 1959.***

"Is the American Family in Danger?" U.S. *News & World
Report,* April 16, 1973.***

Jacoby, Susan. " 'What Do I Do for the Next 20 Years?'
Feminism in the $12,000-a-Year Family." *New York
Times Magazine,* June 17, 1973.**

Janeway, Elizabeth. *Man's World, Woman's Place.* New York:
Morrow, 1971.***

Jeanniere, Abel. *The Anthropology of Sex.* New York: Harper and Row, 1967.*

Johnson, Roger. *Aggression in Man and Animals.* Philadelphia and London: Saunders, 1972.**

Jourard, Sidney. *The Transparent Self.* Princeton, N.J.: Van Nostrand Reinhold, 1964.**

Kahn, Herman. "Sin and Sex in Our Society." *Single,* August 1973.**

Kaiser, Robert Blair. "Sandstone—A Love Community." *Penthouse,* September 1972.**

Katz, Elia. *Armed Love: Inside America's Communes.* New York: Bantam, 1972.*

Kennedy, Eugene C. *The New Sexuality: Myths, Fables and Hang-ups.* New York: Doubleday, 1972.

Key, Mary. "The Role of Male and Female in Children's Books—Dispelling All Doubt." *Wilson Library Bulletin,* October 1971.

Kirkendall, Lester, and Whitehurst, Robert, eds. *The New Sexual Revolution.* New York: Donald Brown, 1971.**

Klein, Carole. *The Single Parent Experience.* Chicago: Walker, 1973.**

Lawrence, Raymond. "The Affair as a Redemptive Experience: A Case Study." In Robert H. Rimmer, ed., *Adventures in Loving.****

————. "Flexible Monogamy: The Uncharted Territory." In Robert H. Rimmer, ed., *Adventures in Loving.****

————. "Toward a More Flexible Monogamy." *Christianity and Crisis,* March 16, 1974.***

Lear, Martha. "The Case for Loving Just One Man." *Redbook,* August 1973.**

Lee, C. T. "Reactions of Mouse Fighters to Male and Female Mice, Intact or Deodorized." *American Zoologist* 10 (1970):56.*

Leonard, George B. *The Transformation: A Guide to the Inevitable Changes in Humankind.* New York: Delacorte, 1972.**

————. "Why We Need a New Sexuality." *Look,* January 13, 1970.**

Lewinsohn, Richard. *A History of Sexual Customs, from Earliest Times to the Present.* New York: Harper and Row, 1971.**

Lewis, C. S. *The Allegory of Love: A Study of Medieval Tradition.* Oxford: Oxford University Press, 1936.*

Libby, Roger, and Whitehurst, Robert, eds. *Renovating Marriage: Toward New Sexual Life Styles.* Danville, Calif.: Consensus Press, 1973.***

Lobell, John, and Lobell, Mimi. *John & Mimi: A Free Marriage.* New York: St. Martin's Press, 1972.**

Lorenz, Konrad. *On Aggression.* Translated by Marjorie K. Wilson. New York: Harcourt Brace Jovanovich, 1966.*

McClintock, Martha. "Menstrual Synchrony and Suppression." *Nature* (London), January 22, 1971.*

McGrady, Patrick. *The Love Doctors.* New York: Macmillan, 1972.*

MacLean, Paul. "The Brain's Generation Gap: Some Human Implications." *Zygon,* June 1973.*

McLuhan, Marshall, and Leonard, George B. "The Future of Sex." *Look,* July 25, 1967.

Marshall, Donald, and Suggs, Robert, eds. *Human Sexual Behavior: Variations across the Ethnographic Spectrum.* Englewood Cliffs, N.J.: Prentice-Hall, 1971.*

Maslow, Abraham. *Eupsychian Management: A Journal.* Homewood, Ill.: Irwin and Dorsey Press, 1965.**

———. *Motivation and Personality.* New York: Harper and Row, 1954.***

———. *New Knowledge in Human Values.* Chicago: Henry Regnery, 1970.*

———. *The Psychology of Science: A Reconnaissance.* New York: Harper and Row, 1966.**

———. *Toward a Psychology of Being.* 2nd ed. New York: Van Nostrand Reinhold, 1968.**

Maslow, Abraham, and Honigmann, John, eds. "Synergy: Some Notes of Ruth Benedict." *American Anthropologist* 72 (1970):320–333.***

May, Rollo. *Love and Will.* New York: Norton, 1969.**

————. *Power and Innocence: A Search for the Sources of Violence.* New York: Norton, 1972.

Mead, Margaret. *Culture and Commitment: A Study of the Generation Gap.* Garden City, N.Y.: Natural History Press, 1970.**

————. *Growing Up in New Guinea.* New York: Dell, 1968.**

————. "A Next Step in Being a Woman." *Redbook,* August 1973.**

————. *Sex and Temperament in Three Primitive Societies.* New York: Dell, 1967.**

Menard, Wilmon. "Love Marquesan Style." *Sexual Behavior,* September 1972.

Milhaven, John G. *Toward a New Catholic Morality.* New York: Doubleday, 1970.*

Money, John, and Ehrhardt, Anke. *Man and Woman, Boy and Girl.* Baltimore: Johns Hopkins University Press, 1972.*

Montagu, Ashley. *Touching: The Human Significance of the Skin.* New York and London: Columbia University Press, 1971.**

Morris, Desmond. *The Human Zoo.* New York: Dell, 1971.*

————. *Intimate Behaviour.* New York: Random House, 1972.*

————. *The Naked Ape.* New York: McGraw-Hill, 1968.*

Morrison, Eleanor, and Borosage, Vera. *Human Sexuality: Contemporary Perspectives.* Palo Alto, Calif.: National Press Books, 1973.*

Mugford, R. A., and Nowell, N. W. "The Preputial Glands as a Source of Aggression-Promoting Odors in Mice." *Physiological Behavior* 6 (1971):247–249.*

Murdock, G. P. *Social Structures.* New York: Macmillan, 1949.*

Neubeck, Gerhard P., ed. *Extramarital Relations.* Englewood Cliffs, N.J.: Prentice-Hall, 1969.***

O'Brien, Denise. "Female Husbands in African Societies." A paper delivered at the annual meeting of the American Anthropological Association, December 1972.*

O'Neill, Nena, and O'Neill, George. "Is Your Marriage Chang-
ing More Than You Realize?" *Family Circle,* January
1973.**
———. *Open Marriage: A New Life Style for Couples.* New
York: M. Evans, 1972.***
———. "Open Marriage for Singles." *Single,* August 1973.**
———. "Patterns in Group Sexual Activity." *Journal of Sex
Research,* May 1970.*
Otto, Herbert A., ed. *The Family in Search of a Future: Alter-
nate Models for Moderns.* New York: Appleton-Cen-
tury-Crofts, 1970.**
———. "Man-Woman Relationships in the Society of the Fu-
ture." *The Futurist,* April 1973.
Overholser, Charles. "Marriage 1973 Style." *Family Circle,*
February 1973.*
Packard, Vance. *A Nation of Strangers.* New York: McKay,
1972.**
———. *The Sexual Wilderness.* New York: McKay, 1968.**
Padovano, Anthony. *Free to Be Faithful.* New York: Paulist-
Newman, 1972.*
Peterman, Dan. "Towards Interpersonal Fulfillment in an
Eupsychian Culture." *Journal of Humanistic Psychol-
ogy,* Spring 1972.***
Peters, Victor. *All Things Common: The Hutterian Way of
Life.* New York: Harper and Row, 1971.
Peterson, Joyce, and Mercer, Marilyn. *Adultery for Adults.*
New York: Bantam, 1968.
Pittenger, William Norman. *Making Sexuality Human.* Phila-
delphia: United Church Press, 1970.*
Poor, Riva. *4 Days, 40 Hours: Reporting a Revolution in
Work and Leisure.* Cambridge, Mass.: Bursk and Poor,
1970.*
Rachewiltz, Boris De. *Black Eros: The Sexual Customs of
Africa from Prehistory to the Present Day.* Translated
by Peter Whigham. New York: Lyle Stuart, 1964.**
Rapoport, Rhona, and Rapoport, Robert. *Dual-Career Fami-
lies.* Baltimore: Penguin, 1972.**

Reich, Charles A. *The Greening of America.* New York: Bantam, 1971.**

Reich, Wilhelm. *The Sexual Revolution: Toward a Self-governing Character Structure.* Translated by Terese Pol. New York: Farrar, Straus and Giroux, 1971.*

Reicke, Reimut. *Sexuality and Class Struggle.* New York: Praeger, 1971.

Reisinger, Joseph. "Legal Pitfalls of Living Together." *Single,* August 1973.*

Richardson, Herbert W. *Nun, Witch, Playmate: The Americanization of Sex.* New York: Harper and Row, 1971.***

Riegel, Robert. *American Women: A Story of Social Change.* Rutherford, N.J.: Fairleigh Dickinson University Press, 1970.*

Rimmer, Robert H. *The Harrad Experiment.* New York: Bantam, 1967.***

————. *Proposition Thirty-one.* New York: New American Library, 1969.***

————. *The Rebellion of Yale Marratt.* New York: Avon, 1967.***

————. *Thursday, My Love.* New York: New American Library, 1972.***

————. ed. *Adventures in Loving.* New York: New American Library, 1973.***

————. ed. *The Harrad Letters to Robert H. Rimmer.* New York: New American Library, 1969.***

————. ed. *You and I Searching for Tomorrow.* New York: New American Library, 1971.***

Robertson, Constance Noyes, ed. *Oneida Community: An Autobiography, 1851–1876.* Syracuse: Syracuse University Press, 1970.**

Robinson, John A. T. *Christian Freedom in a Permissive Society.* Philadelphia: Westminster, 1970.*

Rogers, Carl. *Becoming Partners: Marriage and Its Alternatives.* New York: Delacorte, 1972.***

Ropartz, P. "The Relation Between Olfactory Stimulation and Aggressive Behavior in Mice." *Animal Behavior,* 16 (1968):97–100.*

Roszak, Betty, and Roszak, Theodore, eds. *Masculine/Feminine: Readings in Sexual Mythology and the Liberation of Women.* New York: Harper and Row, 1969.**

Roy, Rustum, and Roy, Della. *Honest Sex.* New York: New American Library, 1968.***

———. "Is Monogamy Outdated?" *The Humanist,* March–April 1970.

Ruether, Rosemary Radford. "The Ethic of Celibacy." *Commonweal,* February 2, 1973.

———. *Liberation Theology.* New York: Paulist-Newman, 1973.***

———. "Nature, Fall and Reconciliation in the Theology of Women's Liberation"; "Female Language in God-talk and the Significance of Mariology in Christian Theology"; "The Ideology of Feminity in Protestantism and Bourgeois Family Life"; "The Roots of Female Subjugation in Western Religious Ideology and Social Development"; and "The Role of Asceticism in the Subjugation and Liberation of Women." Five unpublished lectures given at Drew University, Madison, N.J., in April 1973.

Scanzoni, John. *Sexual Bargaining: Power Politics in the American Marriage.* Englewood Cliffs, N.J.: Prentice-Hall, 1972.**

Schillebeeckx, Edward. *Marriage: Human Reality and Saving Mystery.* New York: Sheed and Ward, 1965.

Schulz, David. *The Changing Family: Its Function and Future.* Englewood Cliffs, N.J.: Prentice-Hall, 1972.*

Scott, Valerie [pseud.]. *Surrogate Wife.* New York: Dell, 1971.

Singer, Irving. *The Goals of Human Sexuality.* New York: Norton, 1973.

Smith, Page. *Daughters of the Promised Land: Women in American History.* Boston: Little, Brown, 1970.**

Snoek, C. Jaime. "Marriage and the Institutionalization of Sexual Relations." In Franz Böckle, ed., *The Future of Marriage as an Institution.* New York: Herder and Herder, 1970.**

Sorensen, Robert C. *Adolescent Sexuality in Contemporary America: Personal Values and Sexual Behavior Ages Thirteen to Nineteen.* rev. ed. New York: World, 1973.**

Taylor, Gordon Rattray. *Rethink: A Paraprimitive Solution.* New York: Dutton, 1973.***

————. *Sex in History.* London: Thames and Hudson, 1954.***

Thorp, Roderick, and Blake, Robert. *Wives: An Investigation.* New York: M. Evans, 1971.*

Tiger, Lionel. *Men in Groups.* New York: Random House, 1970.*

Tiger, Lionel, and Fox, Robin. *The Imperial Animal.* New York: Holt, Rinehart and Winston, 1971.*

Toffler, Alvin. *Future Shock.* New York: Random House, 1970.***

United Presbyterian Church in the U.S.A. *Sexuality and the Human Community.* Philadelphia: United Presbyterian Church in the U.S.A., 1970.***

Van der Poel, Cornelius. *The Search for Human Values.* New York: Paulist-Newman, 1971.*

Van der Zee, John. *Canyon: The Story of the Last Rustic Community in Metropolitan America.* New York: Harcourt Brace Jovanovich, 1971.

Voorhies, Barbara. "Supernumerary Sexes." A paper presented at the annual meeting of the American Anthropological Association, December 1972.*

Wassmer, Thomas A., and Fletcher, Joseph. *Hello Lovers! An Invitation to Situation Ethics.* Washington, D.C.: Corpus, 1970.**

Watts, Alan. *Nature, Man and Woman.* New York: Random House, 1970.**

Wickler, Wolfgang. *The Biology of the Ten Commandments.* Translated by David Smith. New York: McGraw-Hill, 1972.*

————. *The Sexual Code: The Social Behavior of Animals and Men.* Translated by Francisca Garvie. New York: Doubleday, 1972.*

Williamson, John. *Project Synergy: An Outline and Abstract.* Topanga, Calif.: Sandstone Foundation, 1970.**

————. *Sexuality and Social Stability.* Topanga, Calif.: Sandstone Foundation, 1970.**

Wilson, James, et al. "Modification in the Sexual Behavior of Male Rats Produced by Changing the Stimulus Female." *Journal of Comparative and Physiological Psychology* 56 (1963):636–644.*

Winick, Charles. *The New People: Desexualization in American Life.* New York: Pegasus, 1968.**

Winter, Gibson. *Love and Conflict: New Patterns in Family Life.* New York: Doubleday, 1958.**

Wolfe, Linda. "Can Adultery Save Your Marriage?" *Cosmopolitan,* January 1973.**

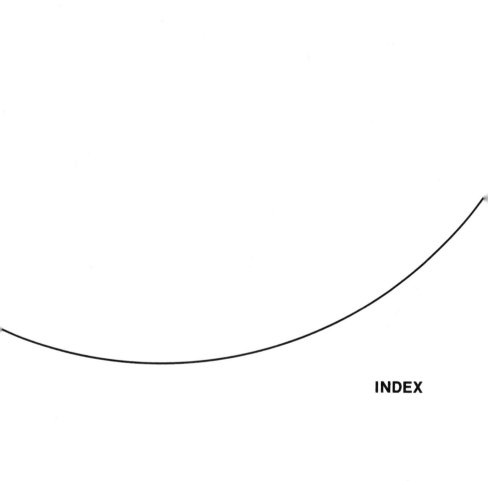

INDEX